# Migration Law in Greece

# Migration Law in Greece

**Konstantinos D. Magliveras**

This book was originally published as a monograph in the International Encyclopaedia of Laws/Migration Law.

Founding Editor: Roger Blanpain
General Editor: Frank Hendrickx
Volume Editor: Helen Oosterom-Staples

Wolters Kluwer

*Published by:*
Kluwer Law International B.V.
PO Box 316
2400 AH Alphen aan den Rijn
The Netherlands
E-mail: lrs-sales@wolterskluwer.com
Website: www.wolterskluwer.com/en/solutions/kluwerlawinternational

*Sold and distributed by:*
Wolters Kluwer Legal & Regulatory U.S.
920 Links Avenue
Landisville, PA 17538
United States of America
E-mail: customer.service@wolterskluwer.com



ISBN 978-94-035-4439-7

e-Book: ISBN 978-94-035-4449-6
web-PDF: ISBN 978-94-035-4459-5

# The Author

Konstantinos D. Magliveras, D. Phil (Oxon), is an attorney at law, and member of the Athens Bar Association.

## The Author

# Table of Contents

**Table of Contents**

# List of Abbreviations

| | |
|---|---|
| ATV | Airport Transit Visa |
| CCP | Code of Criminal Procedure |
| CETS | Council of Europe Treaty Series |
| CJEU | Court of Justice of the European Union |
| Doc. | Document |
| EAW | European Arrest Warrant |
| ECHR | Convention for the Protection of Human Rights and Fundamental Freedoms |
| ECtHR | European Court of Human Rights |
| EEA | European Economic Area |
| EFSF | European Financial Stability Facility |
| EFTA | European Free Trade Association |
| ESCO | European Skills, Competences, Qualifications and Occupations |
| ETIAS | European Travel Information and Authorization System |
| ETS | European Treaty Series |
| EU | European Union |
| EUAA | European Union Agency for Asylum |
| FEK | Gazette of the Hellenic Government |
| FRO | Fundamental Rights Officer |
| ILO | International Labour Organization |
| ISCO | International Standard Classification of Occupation |
| MoU | Memorandum of Understanding |
| O.J. | Official Journal |
| PACE | Council of Europe's Parliamentary Assembly |
| SIS | Schengen Information System |
| SPOC | Single Point of Contact |

**List of Abbreviations**

| | |
|---|---|
| TEU | Treaty on European Union |
| TFEU | Treaty on the Functioning of the European Union |
| THB | Trafficking in Human Beings |
| UN | United Nations |
| UNTS | United Nations Treaty Series |

# Preface

This is the second edition of *Migration Law in Greece*, the monograph originally appeared in 2010. The Preface of the first edition noted that the waves of (mostly irregular) immigration in Greece in the closing years of the 1980s and during the first half of the 1990s had not been handled in a well-organized and efficient manner. It was also noted that the Greek State was not able to come up with an appropriate legislative framework so as to reap the benefits of immigration while guaranteeing the orderly participation and integration of foreigners in Greek society.

During the second decade of the twenty-first century, Greece found itself embroiled in what has been called the '2015–2016 European migrant crisis', namely the arrival of 1.3 million refugees and irregular migrants originating mostly from countries in Asia and having used Turkey as a transit country. The increased number of arrivals made clear that Greece was unable to deal with these migratory waves on its own. However, as the external borders of Greece are at the same time the external borders of the European Union (EU), the matter automatically became an issue to be dealt with by the EU. The latter, by using various tools and mechanisms, including effective border management schemes, pursued its foreign policy goals with the countries of origin and transit. From a monetary point of view, this migration crisis has been costly for the EU (some EUR 17.7 billion was allocated from the EU budget to deal with it in the period 2015–2017, while EUR 22.7 billion has been reserved for migration and border management in the EU budget for the period 2021–2027). It was, nevertheless, the cost of inter-Member States relations that questioned solidarity and the ability to handle promptly, efficiently and effectively increased arrivals from outside the EU borders.

Greece was principally an EU transit country for the third-country nationals to reach other EU Member States. Greece has been criticized for the treatment of and conduct towards asylum seekers in the so-called hotspots (the official designation is 'Closed Controlled Access Centres'), where they are held during the evaluation of their applications for refugee status. The European Court of Human Rights (ECtHR) has concluded in a number of cases that the conditions in 'hotspots' amounted to inhumane and degrading treatment in violation of the (European) Convention for the Protection of Human Rights and Fundamental Freedoms (ECHR).[1]

1. *See* ECtHR, *A.D. v. Greece*, Application No. 55363/19, Judgment of 4 Apr. 2023; ECtHR, *M.L. v. Greece*, Application No. 8386/20, Judgment of 23 Nov. 2023; ECtHR, *M.B. v. Greece*, Application No. 8389/20, Judgment of 23 Nov. 2023, all available at: https://www.echr.coe.int/ Greece has

## Preface

If there is one thing that characterizes the Greek legislation on migration, it is that it is constantly in the process of being completed, amended, or revised and, perhaps too often, substituted with new and more appropriate laws. The required regulatory stability and permanency have almost never existed. Each overhaul of the relevant legislation has been accompanied by the expectation that finally, the new regulatory regime will endure many years to come, only to be disappointed. It remains to be seen whether the current Immigration Code (Law 5038/2023), which came into operation on 31 March 2024, will turn out to be the efficient and effective legislative instrument that an EU Member State (effectively a country of the First World) should have in place. The reference to the EU is not made here without good reason. This is because many aspects of the migration process from third countries to the EU territory as well as of the residence of foreigners in the Member States as host countries are part of EU law. To put it otherwise, in all the current twenty-seven Member States there are uniform rules, norms and procedures to deal with those third-country nationals (to use the EU terminology) who leave their country and come to work, provide services, study, invest, etc., in one of the countries of the most integrated international organization in the world.

As no doubt the reader will soon ascertain, the single largest number of provisions in the Immigration Code are provisions transposing the relevant EU law into the Greek legal system or harmonizing the latter with the former. Every time the relevant EU law is amended or every time a new EU legal instrument pertaining to immigration (broadly defined) is adopted, the Immigration Code will have to change accordingly. An observant reader might ask the following question: Since EU law plays such a dominating role in the regulation of almost all aspects of immigration, why has been argued above that the Greek legislation is in a state of constant flux?

Even though prima faciae this appears to be a quite straightforward question, the answer is anything but easy. Arguably, there are two principal reasons. The first reason is that, generally speaking, there has never been continuity and permanence in the public administration, throughout the 200 years of history of the contemporary Hellenic State. Each new government is convinced that it has the right policies and strategies, which is enough justification to change the existing rules and introduce new ones. Unfortunately, it is more often the case than not that the new rules prove inadequate or ineffective in addressing the situation; the government in power will attempt to correct them and to re-balance and this could continue *ad infinatum*. The second reason is that Greek governments have never managed to deal with the very serious problem of irregular immigration.

During the last decade or so, the notion of irregular immigrants has been rather confused with asylum seekers and the victims of trafficking. It is submitted that these are distinct categories of third-country nationals and, consequently, they should be treated differently. Moreover, it is relatively easy to enter into the Greek territory undetected and also to remain therein without being spotted for many years. With a coastline exceeding 13,600 kilometres and with over 2,000 islands,

ratified the ECHR twice: originally when it became the eleventh member of the Council of Europe on 9 Aug. 1949 and which was repudiated when Greece withdrew from the Council of Europe in 1970 and, again, in November 1974, after Greece was re-admitted, pursuant to Legislative Decree 53/1974, *see* Table of Greek Legislation.

entering Greece and remaining in its territory without a right to do so is relatively easy. And if one is arrested for doing so, one can always claim to be a refugee and apply to be granted asylum.

As was mentioned in the Preface of the present monograph's first edition, it was at the time the only comprehensive analysis of the relevant Greek legislation in a foreign language. Fifteen years later, to the best of this author's knowledge, it still is the only available treatise on the subject. This is regrettable. But it is also regrettable that the current Immigration Code has still not been translated into a foreign language. It can only be hoped that the present monograph will introduce the Greek law on immigration and asylum to a wider audience and will assist both researchers and professionals in understanding and applying this often-cumbersome legislation.

Finally, a word on the continuity of this, second edition of the monograph. The first chapter, which is titled 'Domestic legal instruments pertaining to the regulation of immigration' also has the purpose of informing the readers of the first edition of what has happened in the meantime in the regulation of immigration in Greece, in particular, which legislative instruments have been adopted and to elaborate on problems and challenges that had to be addressed and resolved during the previous fifteen years.[2]

All translations in the present monograph have been made by the author. The use of the male adjective also includes the female adjective and vice versa, unless otherwise mentioned.

*November 2024*
*Konstantinos D. Magliveras*

2. As regards the top priorities in the national migration policy state in 2022, *see* Ministry of Migration & Asylum, First International Migration Review Forum on the UN Global Compact for Safe, Orderly and Regular Migration, 'Voluntary GCM Review by Greece', May 2022, at: https://migrationnetwork.un.org/system/files/docs/GREECE%20-%20Voluntary%20GCM%20Review.pdf.

# General Introduction

## §1. Domestic Legal Instruments Pertaining to the Regulation of Irregular Immigration

### I. Legal Instruments Pertaining to Immigration

*1.* The first Greek legislation that dealt specifically with aliens and foreign residents was Law 4310/1929.[3] Having been repeatedly amended and revised, it had a life span that exceeded sixty years. It was abrogated when Law 1975/1991 was promulgated.[4] It constituted the first legislative instrument to address and manage the immigration waves that were flowing into the Greek territory when Europe, and especially South East Europe and the Balkans as far as Greece was concerned, was experiencing the consequences of the geo-political developments of the time (the end of the Cold War, the disintegration of the Federal Socialist Republic of Yugoslavia and of the Union of Soviet Socialist Republics, as well as globalization). More specifically, Law 1975/1991 was an attempt to deal with the serious challenges that had been created by mass immigration, which was mostly irregular, a novelty for both the Greek State and for the Greek society at large.

*2.* The application of Law 1975/1991, which was drafted in haste, proved to be ineffective in tackling migratory flows from neighbouring countries, with people looking for work, in a very affluent, by regional standards, Greece – already a Member State of the European Economic Community. It failed to deal with the hundreds of thousands of illegal and undocumented migrant workers, who very quickly became part of Greece's ever-booming informal employment market. This raised the multifaceted challenges of these irregular immigrants' future, as they started

3. Law 4310/1929, Establishment and movement of aliens in Greece, police controls, passports, deportations and displacements, Gazette of the Hellenic Government (hereinafter 'FEK') 1929 Issue A' No. 287. Note that the official name of Greece is the *Hellenic Republic*, the name of the country is *Hellas*, and the people are called *Hellenes*. However, as the terms 'Greece' and 'Greek' have prevailed internationally, it is with some regret that they are used in the present monograph. The words 'Hellas', 'Hellenic', etc., have been employed when it was considered to be more appropriate. Moreover, for purposes of explication, the Official Gazette of the Hellenic Government (abbreviated here as 'FEK') is the official State publication where all laws, presidential decrees, ministerial decisions, and other acts are compulsory published. Any law that has been promulgated according to the Constitution but has not been published in the Official Gazette is null and void. The Official Gazette can be consulted at: https://search.et.gr/en/.
4. Law 1975/1991, Entry, exit, stay, employment, deportation of aliens, procedure for recognition of foreign refugees and other provisions, FEK 1991 Issue A' No. 184.

their own families. Thus, the question of legalizing their stay, in other words to have them registered, to issue them with residence permits as well as to grant work permits to those who qualified, was a legislative priority and a challenge for a rather backwards-looking public administration. Very shortly, it became an administrative nightmare, arguably because Greece, as a state institution and as a population, has never really managed to understand and process the global and regional transformations that have taken place from the late 1980s onwards.

*3.* In the course of 1998, a new system for the legalization of irregular aliens was implemented,[5] which for some bizarre reason, ran in parallel with the system that already existed, namely the one pursuant to Law 1975/1991. The new system introduced the so-called green card. It was meant to offer irregular and undocumented aliens a legal title to lawful residence and employment. More than 370,000 migrant workers took advantage of this 'amnesty' and participated in the new system which, *inter alia*, aimed at registering all aliens, who had entered the Greek territory and resided illegally (they came principally from Albania and from the former Soviet Union). Even though around 210,000–220,000 aliens were successful in being granted residence and work permits ('green cards'), which regularized their status in Greece as well as that of family members, the scheme was regarded as a failure primarily because it had no appreciable effect in curbing irregular immigration, which continued to increase.

*4.* An(other) overhaul of the immigration regulation and policy was carried out in 2001. It led to the promulgation of Law 2910/2001,[6] which introduced a second scheme for regularizing irregular immigrants. Even though some 350,000 aliens applied for regularization and, finally, around 228,000 residence permits were issued, this figure should not be added *in toto* to the number of aliens, who had successfully registered under the 1998 scheme. It is widely believed that a considerable (but undefined) number of those granted a permit under the 1998 scheme had in the meantime become undocumented aliens and, consequently, they re-registered under the provisions of Law 2910/2001. Moreover, there appear to have been cases where properly documented immigrants registered again under the new regime either because they were not informed differently or because they thought that, by doing so, they would extend the duration of the residence permits that they already possessed.[7] The application of Law 2910/2001 showed many deficiencies, which necessitated no less than thirteen amendments and revisions until 2004, when the government of the day resolved that a new immigration policy should be adopted and that the applicable legislative regime should, yet again, be overhauled.

5. Only for historical interest, the system was put into operation under Presidential Decree 358/1997 and Presidential Decree 359/1997.
6. Law 2910/2001, Entry and residence of aliens in the Greek territory, acquisition of Greek citizenship by naturalization and other provisions, FEK 2001 Issue A' No. 91. For commentary, *see* G. Papagianni and P. Naskou-Perraki, 'Greece', in I. Higgins (ed.), *Migration and Asylum Law and Policy in the European Union: FIDE 2004 National Reports* (Cambridge: Cambridge University Press, 2005) 135.
7. Note that the system devised under Law 2910/2001 lacked the necessary mechanism to automatically exclude from registration those aliens Law who were in good standing.

5. The result was Law 3386/2005, which entered into force on 1 January 2006.[8] Soon afterwards, it was amended twice,[9] a year later it was thoroughly revised,[10] and in its revised form, it was further modified four times.[11] In the course of the years 2005 to 2007, a third programme of mass regularization of irregular aliens was carried out. It led to the issuance of around 96,000 residence permits in 2006 and another 20,000 permits in 2007. Even though the numbers were significantly smaller compared to the previous two programmes of legalization, they were still quite significant considering that, at the time, the total number of foreigners living in Greece was thought to be around 1 million, roughly 10% of the population.[12]

6. To summarize developments in the regulation of immigration during the crucial period 1990–2010, it is perhaps best to quote from the explanatory memorandum that accompanied the introduction of draft Law 3838/2010 into Parliament:

> About twenty years ago, the country was overwhelmed by the first wave of immigrants in its post-war history, as thousands of people mostly from neighbouring Albania entered Greece en masse and without any formalities, taking advantage of the border policy which had been adopted by the then government. Subsequently, the difficulties of designing effective immigration policies combined with [Greece's] endemic underground economy made our country a magnet for illegal [migrant] workers for years, resulting in the creation of a permanent and ever-growing population living on the fringes of social life and legality. Attempts in previous years to deal with the situation by setting new rules did not yield substantial results. The[se attempts] sought to gain control of the situation by the mass legalization of those who were already living and working illegally in the country. The automatic and massive legalizations, which were also implemented by other European states, obliged the organs of the EU to include the explicit and strict rejection of such options in the European Pact on Migration and Asylum.[13] It is clear that, in view of the change in immigration flows, the legalization policy, especially in its most recent version, has not contributed to the elimination of illegal immigration. On the contrary, it has blurred the distinction between legal and illegal residence and

8. Law 3386/2005, Entry, residence and social integration of third-country nationals into the Greek territory, FEK 2005 Issue A' No. 212. For detailed analysis of Law 3386/2005, as was in force at the end of 2009, with more historical references to the Greek immigration legislation, *see* K. Magliveras, *Migration Law in Greece* (Alphen aan den Rijn: Wolters Kluwer, 2011).
9. Under Law 3448/2006, FEK 2006 Issue A' No. 57, and under Law 3491/2006, FEK 2006 Issue A' No. 207.
10. Under Law 3536/2007, Special arrangements for immigration policy issues and other matters falling into the competence of the Ministry of the Interior, Public Administration and Decentralization, FEK 2007 Issue A' No. 42.
11. Under Law 3613/2007, FEK 2007 Issue A' No. 263; Law 3731/2008, FEK 2008 Issue A' No. 263; Law 3772/2009, FEK 2009 Issue A' No. 112; and Law 3801/2009, FEK 2009 Issue A' No. 163.
12. Generally, *see* M. Baldwin-Edwards, 'Greece' in M. Baldwin-Edwards and A. Kraler (eds), *REGINE: Regularisations in Europe* (Pallas Publications & European Commission/Amsterdam University Press, Amsterdam 2009) 297–330.
13. The reference is to the following document: Council of the European Union, *European Pact on Migration and Asylum*, 13440/08, Brussels, 24 Sep. 2008, available at: https://data.consilium.europa.eu/doc/document/ST-13440-2008-INIT/en/pdf.

employment and has created expectations that would be repeated periodically and would act as an incentive for new [illegal migratory] flows.

*7.* What transpires from the above extract and what the countless changes and amendments no doubt show[14] is that for over twenty years Greece has been unable to adopt, maintain and adhere to a specific immigration policy and to regulate all aspects of migration accordingly. On the contrary, immigration has become a topic dominated by the political orientation and ideology of the government that was each time in power. But the continued inability to put in place a legal mechanism with the appropriate procedures, which, at the same time, would have satisfied the rights of immigrants and would have taken into account the opinion and the attitude of citizens vis-à-vis immigration (and specifically illegal migration flows), could reveal that Greece suffers from a problematic rule of law and faces difficulties in functioning as a First World country. Arguably, it is a sign of a country where the rule of law operates as it should to be able to have in place a set of regulations and processes that ensure the protection of not only the rights of migrants vis-à-vis the State but also the rights of the State vis-à-vis migrants.

*8.* In 2014, amid the fiscal and economic crisis, the Greek Parliament abrogated the aforementioned Law 3386/2005 on immigration and adopted Law 4251/2014, whose title was 'Immigration and Social Integration Code'.[15] It was published in the Official Gazette of the Hellenic Government on 1 April 2014 and entered into force two months later. Law 4251/2014 resulted in important reforms as regards the residence permits issued to foreigners as well as their social integration, although the latter rather remained a dead letter as apparently none of the actions envisaged therein has been implemented.

*9.* The main changes that Law 4251/2014 brought to the legislation on immigration could be summarized as follows:

a. those foreigners holding valid residence permits were offered the opportunity to be employed (effectively to become 'migrant workers');

---

14. Note that, during the 2010s, Law 3386/2005 was amended (also for the need to incorporate/adapt certain EU legislation into the Greek legal order) by Law 3907/2011 (FEK 2011 Issue A' No. 7, *see infra*), by Law 4018/2011 (FEK 2011 Issue A' No. 215), by Law 4071/2012 (FEK 2012 Issue A' No. 85) and by Law 4146/2013 (FEK 2013 Issue A' No. 90).
15. FEK 2014 Issue A' No. 80. Note that Law 4251/2014 had been amended several times, e.g., by Law 4332/2015, Amendment of the provisions of the Greek Citizenship Code – Amendment of Law 4251/2014 for the adaptation of the Greek legislation to the directives of the European Parliament and of the Council 2011/98/EU regarding the single procedure for submitting an application for the granting of a single residence permit to citizens of third countries and of work in the territory of a Member State and on a common set of rights for workers from third countries legally residing in a Member State and 2014/36/EU on the conditions of entry and residence of citizens of third countries for the purpose of seasonal work and other provisions, FEK 2015 Issue A' No. 76. For an overview, *see* International Organization for Migration/Mission to Greece, 'Migration legal guide for practitioners in Greece', September 2017, at: https://greece.iom.int/sites/g/files/tmzbdl1086/files/documents/IOM%20Legal%20Guide_English.pdf.

b. foreigners were also allowed to be engaged in self-employment, a right whose exercise required the possession of a long-term residence permit;
c. foreigners, who were in legal residence, were offered the opportunity to change the purpose of their stay and to obtain the so-called EU Blue Card (on which *see infra*). The purpose of this amendment was to deal with the situation that had arisen concerning third-country nationals, who had come to Greece for studies, and were not able to continue residing legally once their studies had been completed;
d. as regards the conditions for family reunification, the obligation for the head of the family to prove sufficient financial means during the process of renewing the residence permits of the members of his family was deleted;
e. short-term residence permits were replaced by a national visa offering the right to employment to a broad range of foreigners, including seasonal workers, fishermen, members of artistic groups, those who were already legally employed in another EU Member State or in the European Economic Area (EEA)[16] and had moved to Greece to offer their services (employee inter-company transfers), etc.

*10.* Finally, it was the purpose of Law 4251/2014 to incorporate into the Greek legal order relevant EU secondary legislation, a task that ought to have already been carried out. In this regard, two important points should be made. The first point is that Greece is notoriously late in transposing and implementing compulsory EU legislation into domestic law. For example, EU Directive 2011/51 dealing with the beneficiaries of international protection[17] was transposed into domestic law order in June 2014 (i.e., when Law 4251/2014 entered into force)[18] even though it had to be transposed at the latest before May 2013.[19] The second point has to do with the legislative technique in transposing and/or adapting EU secondary legislation on immigration to the Greek legal order. More specifically, while ordinarily EU legislation is implemented in domestic law either by laws or by presidential decrees, in the case of new or amended EU legislation on immigration, transposition would have taken place in the text of Law 4251/2014. This legislative technique was presumably based on the understanding that, as Law 4251/2014 embodied the Immigration and Social Integration Code, this constituted the corpus of all legal portions and procedures relating to immigration; therefore, any changes, amendments, additions, etc., that had to be implemented because of EU law, would be made to the text of the Code in question. Thus, if the EU were to amend its rules on third-country nationals, who come into a Member State to be employed as highly qualified workforce (*see infra*), as regards Greece, the (compulsory) changes to the domestic legislation will be made to the text of the Immigration Code, as it will be in force at the time. Equally, if the EU were to adopt rules and procedures to regulate a new aspect of

16. The EEA consists of the each time Member States of the European Union and three members of the European Free Trade Association (EFTA), namely Iceland, Liechtenstein and Norway. The fourth EFTA member, Switzerland, is not part of the EEA, which came into existence on 1 Jan. 1994.
17. Directive 2011/51/EU of the European Parliament and of the Council of 11 May 2011 amending Council Directive 2003/109/EC to extend its scope to beneficiaries of international protection, O.J. L 132, 19.5.2011, p. 1.
18. *See* Arts 88 et seq. of Law 4251/2014.
19. *See* Art. 2(1) of Directive 2011/51.

the migration process or any other matter relating to it, it would be the Immigration Code that would be amended to incorporate these new rules and procedures. It follows that even if the provisions of the Immigration Code were not changed on the initiative of the Greek government of the day, they would be changed whenever the EU legislation on immigration is amended or revised and whenever new legislation is adopted by the competent EU organs.

*11.* About a year after the promulgation of Law 4251/2014, as was briefly explained in the Preface, Greece started experiencing a large increase in entry of aliens, who were entering the territory via Turkey (transit country) and coming not only from Asia (primarily from Syria and Afghanistan) but also from Africa.[20] It is estimated that in the period 2015–2016, more than 1.3 million aliens entered the Greek territory, principally from the so-called Northeast Aegean islands.[21] However, as the external borders of Greece are simultaneously part of the external borders of the EU, the issue of the third-country nationals coming into Greece en masse became a 'European matter' – requiring European solutions and legal frameworks.

*12.* Two events from that period deserve to be mentioned. The first is the conclusion in March 2016 of the so-called Statement between the members of the European Council[22] and officials from the Republic of Turkey.[23] The second is the establishment in November 2016, for the first time, of a Ministry of Migration Policy.[24] As regards the first event, it should be noted that the legal nature, and consequently, the legal validity of the 'EU-Turkey Statement', which was primarily

20. In the course of 2015, the three main countries of origin of the aliens arriving in Greece were Syria (estimated at 57%), Afghanistan (22%) and Iraq (5%). Generally, *see* J. Zaragoza-Christiani, *Analysing the Causes of the Refugee Crisis and the Key Role of Turkey: Why Now and Why so Many?* (European University Institute Working/Robert Schuman Centre for Advanced Studies Paper 2015/95, 2015), available at: https://cadmus.eui.eu/handle/1814/38226.
21. Generally, *see* M.O. Stephenson Jr. and Y.A. Stivachtis (eds), *Policy and Politics of the Syrian Refugee Crisis in Eastern Mediterranean States: National and Institutional Perspectives* (Bristol: E-International Relations, 2023); K. Kuschminder and J. Waidler, 'At Europe's Frontline: Factors Determining Migrants Decision Making For Onwards Migration from Greece and Turkey' 9 *Migration and Development* (2020) 188–208.
22. The European Council is the organ of the EU responsible for its general political direction and for setting priorities; it should not be confused with the Council of the EU. The European Council comprises the heads of state or government of all Member States, its President and the President of the European Commission.
23. *See* European Council, Press release, 'EU-Turkey statement', 18 Mar. 2016, at: https://www.consilium.europa.eu/en/press/press-releases/2016/03/18/eu-turkey-statement/. Note that the European Commission has been publishing reports on the implementation of the terms of the 'Statement', *see, e.g.*, Report from the Commission to the European Parliament, the European Council and the Council, *Seventh Report on the Progress made in the implementation of the EU-Turkey Statement*, COM(2017) 470, 6 Sep. 2017. Moreover, the 'Statement' has continued to be a focal point of EU – Turkey relations, *see, e.g.*, European Commission, Joint Communication to the European Council, *State of Play of EU – Turkey political, economic and trade relations*, JOIN (2021) 8 final/2, 22 Mar. 2021.
24. Note that its establishment was part of a wider re-organization of ministries in Greece, *see* Presidential Decree 123/2016, Reconstitution and renaming of the Ministry of Administrative Reform and E-Governance, re-establishment of the Ministry of Tourism, establishment of the Ministry of Migration Policy and the Ministry of Digital Policy, Telecommunications and Information, renaming of

addressing 'the migration crisis' that was created by the aforementioned irregular crossings of aliens into Greek territory through Turkey, has raised heated discussions. The present author has argued that, notwithstanding the way it was concluded and the format it has taken, it should be regarded as a bilateral agreement that is subject to international law rules on treaties.[25] The Court of Justice of the EU (CJEU) has categorically stated that it is an agreement or a treaty but has neither explained its precise nature from a legal or regulatory point of view.[26] Taking into account that this was a case where all EU Member States entered into a number of commitments with a third state (Turkey), and therefore there was unanimity on behalf of the EU, it is a rule of international institutional law that, in these circumstances, an international organization may validly act, even if the act is not envisaged or laid down in the constitutive instrument.

*13.* Notwithstanding the true legal nature of the 'Statement' of March 2016, what is of interest is that it contained several provisions that concerned Greece directly and the handling of the aliens who had entered its territory. Suffice to mention the following extracts: 'All new irregular migrants crossing from Turkey into Greek islands as from 20 March 2016 will be returned to Turkey' (this is extracted from the first point of the Statement), 'Turkey and Greece, assisted by EU institutions and agencies, will take the necessary steps and agree any necessary bilateral arrangements' (also extracted from the first point of the Statement), and 'For every Syrian being returned to Turkey from Greek islands, another Syrian will be resettled from Turkey to the EU taking into account the [United Nations] Vulnerability Criteria' (from the second point of the Statement).[27]

*14.* As regards the second event, no doubt the establishment of a separate ministry for migration signified the importance that migration has for Greece, even though there are other matters arguably far more than important (e.g., relations with the EU) for which there is no ministry of its own. An interesting development was the creation of the Fundamental Rights Officer (FRO) at the Ministry of Migration

---

the Ministry of Interior and Administrative Restructuring, the Ministry of Economy, Development and Tourism, and the Ministry of Infrastructure, Transport and Networks, FEK 2016 Issue A' No. 208.

25. *See* K. Magliveras, 'The Question of Turkey's Readmission of Irregular Migrants from Greece and the Legal Nature of the European Union: Turkey Declaration' 65 *Legal Tribune – The Journal of the Athens Bar Association* (2017) 2322–2337 (in Greek).
26. In its Orders of 28 Feb. 2017, the General Court of the CJEU dismissed the actions for annulment, which had been brought by third-country nationals against the 'EU-Turkey Statement' dated 18 Mar. 2016, in three proceedings, namely Case T-192/16, *NF v. European Council* (EU:T:2017:128), Case T-193/16, *NG v. European Council* (EU:T:2017:129); and Case T-257/16, *NM v. European Council* (EU:T:2017:130). The applicants appealed against the dismissal of their actions, but the CJEU rejected the appeals, *see* Joined Cases C-208/17 P to C-210/17 P, *NF and Others v. European Council*, Order (First Chamber), 12 Sep. 2018, ECLI:EU:C:2018:705.
27. On returns, *see* European Court of Auditors, 'Asylum, Relocation and Return of Migrants: Time to Step Up Action to Address Disparities Between Objectives and Results', Special Report No. 24, 2019, at: https://www.eca.europa.eu/Lists/ECADocuments/SR19_24/SR_Migration_management_EN.pdf.

and Asylum.[28] The duty assigned to the FRO, who acts with autonomy and is independent in the performance of his duties, is to handle and examine, at a preliminary stage, complaints lodged by foreigners for alleged violations of human rights during their access to the Greek territory and/or during the reception and/or asylum procedures. It follows that foreigners may submit a complaint to the FRO, if they believe that they have been directly affected by the Greek State's actions or omissions and consider that one or more of their fundamental rights have been violated. If declared admissible, the FRO shall transfer the complaints to the National Transparency Authority[29] or to another competent public authority in accordance with the applicable legislation and will be kept informed of the progress of the complaints. All complaints are treated as confidential.

*15.* Finally, the Immigration and Social Integration Code, as embodied in Law 4251/2014, was amended several times, including under Law 4686/2020[30] and under Law 4825/2021.[31] Finally, it should be mentioned that Law 4251/2014 retained in force a number of provisions from previous legislative instruments.[32]

## II. The Current Principal Legislation: The Immigration Code (Law 5038/2023) an overview

*16.* In April 2023, the Greek Parliament adopted a new Immigration Code (Law 5038/2023)[33] to replace the previous Immigration and Social Integration Code.[34]

---

28. The Fundamental Rights Officer was created by virtue of Art. 49 of Law 4960/2022, National guardianship system and accommodation framework for unaccompanied minors and other provisions pertaining to the Ministry of Migration and Asylum, FEK 2022 Issue A' No. 145.
29. It was established under Law 4622/2019, Organization, operation and transparency of the Government, government bodies and central public administration, FEK 2019 Issue A' No. 133, as a single independent public authority subject to Parliamentary control to act in accordance with international good practices and the requirements of international law by assuming the responsibilities of five State auditing bodies as well as the General Secretariat of Anti-Corruption.
30. Law 4686/2020, Improvement of the immigration legislation, amendment of provisions in Law 4636/2019, in Law 4375/2016 and in Law 4251/2014, and other provisions, FEK 2020 Issue A' No. 96. It brought changes to eleven articles of Law 4251/2014.
31. Law 4825/2021, Reform of procedures for deportations and returns of third-country nationals, attracting investors and digital nomads, issues of residence permits and procedures for granting international protection, provisions of the competence of the Ministry of Migration and Asylum and of the Ministry of Citizen Protection, and other urgent provisions, FEK 2021 Issue A' No. 157.
32. In particular, these were: (a) the provisions of Arts 76, 77, 78, 80, 81, 82, 83 and 89(1)–(3) of the aforementioned Law 3386/2005; (b) the provisions of Art. 15 of the aforementioned Law 3536/2007; (c) the provisions of Presidential Decree 106/2007, which transposed into Greek law the so-called EU Citizens' Rights Directive (*see infra*); (d) Joint Ministerial Decision 23443/2011; and (e) the provisions of Presidential Decree 131/2006, as amended by Presidential Decree 167/2008 and by Presidential Decree 113/2013, but also as it applied to the family reunification of those who are subject to the provisions of the domestic legislation pertaining to the beneficiaries of international protection.
33. FEK 2023 Issue A' No. 81. At the time of writing, it had not been translated in any foreign languages.
34. Note that the provisions of other legislative instruments, which had been retained in power under Law 4251/2014, continue to be in force under Law 5038/2023.

That the words 'social integration' have been dropped from the wording of the new Code should not go unnoticed. Arguably, it reflects the difficulties which the Hellenic Republic and the Greek society face in addressing in a sincere manner the question of the integration of immigrants, whether social, economic, political, cultural, etc. The new Immigration Code, which has 179 articles and covers 116 pages, was meant to enter into force on 1 January 2024. However, as the competent Ministries had not adopted on time the executory legal instruments that were necessary to make the new Immigration Code operative, its entry into force was postponed to 31 March 2024.[35] This was not the first time that legislation regulating migration could not be applied on time because of serious delays in adopting the required (and essential for its application) secondary legal instruments (principally ministerial decisions).

*17.* The apparent inability of the State administration to act promptly and effectively and issue the necessary regulations on time is arguably one of the issues that have plagued the Greek legal order for a very long period of time. Arguably, it is a very worrisome situation, perhaps even a sign of a problematic rule of rule, considering that the so-called principles of good legislation and good law-making do not appear to be observed.[36] As has been argued, Law 5079/2023 is, on the whole, not an example of 'good legislation'.[37] Moreover, one should not overlook the difficulties that the Greek public administration encounters when it has to deal with new legislation, especially *in casu* legislation that affects directly the life and legal status of hundreds of thousands of foreigners. For instance, in August 2024, the foreign languages version of the website of the Ministry of Labour and Social as well as the English version of the website of the Ministry of Migration and Asylum still cited Law 4251/2014 as the applicable primary legislation on immigration![38]

---

35. *See* Art. 97(3) of Law 5079/2023, Organizational and procedural provisions on development, interventions on enhancement of the fair developmental transition and other urgent provisions, FEK 2023 Issue A' No. 215.
36. On 'good legislation', *see* Arts 57–64 of the aforementioned Law 4622/2019. On the basis of these provisions, in May 2020 the Presidency of the Hellenic Government published a not binding *Manual on the Methodology of Legislative Drafting*, which was prepared with the technical support of the European Commission (Directorate General for Structural Reforms) and *Expertise France*, the French public agency mandated to design and implement international technical cooperation projects. Note also that in December 2020, a Better Regulation Office was established as part of the Secretariat General for Legal and Parliamentary Affairs at the Presidency of the Hellenic Government. Generally, *see* Organization for Economic Cooperation and Development, *OECD Regulatory Policy Outlook 2021: Greece*, at: https://www.oecd-ilibrary.org/sites/3022a272-en/index.html?itemId=/content/component/3022a272-en.
37. *See* C. Stilianidou, 'Law 5079/2023 and the Rules of Good Legislation', *Govwatch*, 20 Dec. 2023, at: https://govwatch.gr/en/finds/o-nomos-5079-2023-kai-oi-provlimatismoi-se-epipedo-kalis-nomothetisis/.
38. *See*, respectively, Ministry of Labour and Social Affairs, 'Work for Third-Country Nationals in Greece', at: https://ypergasias.gov.gr/en/labour-relations/individual-employment-relations/work-for-third-country-nationals-in-greece/, and 'Residence Permit Categories for Third Country Citizens & Documents to be Submitted', at: https://migration.gov.gr/en/migration-policy/metanasteusi-stin-ellada/katigories-adeion-diamonis-politon-triton-choron-dikaiologitika%e2%80%8b/, both accessed on 30 Apr. 2025.

*18.* It is also noteworthy that amending Law 5078/2023 contains three other provisions, which are directly related to migration, but which were not included in the text of the Immigration Code, effectively becoming self-standing provisions. The first provision (Article 191 of Law 5078/2023) created two new executive positions in the Ministry of Immigration and Asylum, the first being the 'National Coordinator on Returns' and the second being the 'National Coordinator against Illegal Trafficking of Migrants'. The persons to hold the respective office are appointed by a joint decision of the Minister of Immigration and Asylum and the Minister of Citizen Protection. For both these positions only active or pensioned senior officers of the Hellenic Police are eligible for selection. Whether this provision is in conformity with the Constitution is highly questionable. The second provision (Article 193 of Law 5078/2023), without making any reference to the Immigration Code, introduced a new type of residence permit to be issued to third-country nationals for employment purposes, subject to certain conditions and requirements. This new type of permit should be considered to be additional to those which are envisaged in the Immigration Code; it is analysed *infra.*

*19.* Finally, the third provision (Article 194 of Law 5078/2023), which entered into force on the day the Immigration Code came into force, affords the beneficiaries of temporary international protection the possibility to apply to be issued with a residence permit for one of the categories of residence permits that are envisaged in the Immigration Code.

*20.* At the time of writing, the latest amendment to the Immigration Code was under Law 5130/2024,[39] which brought changes to Article 64 and to Article 65 of Law 5038/2023 (*see infra*).

*21.* The purpose of Law 5038/2023 was to reform the Immigration and Social Integration Code (Law 4251/2014) and to regulate anew the categories of entry visas as well as the types of residence permits that are issued to third-country nationals by the competent Greek authorities. Moreover, it is meant to ensure that the immigration policies are adapted to the current needs of the Greek society and economy and that the relevant procedures are simplified, transparent and efficient. Even though Article 4 of Law 5038/2023 defines no less than eighty words and terms, one would not find definitions for either the term 'immigration' or 'migrant', by which one has in mind 'legal immigration' and 'legal migrant'. To define them

39. *See* Arts 48 and 49 of Law 5130/2024, Strengthening of the control system for the Asset Declarations and the Declarations of Financial Interests envisaged in Law 5026/2023 – Placement of a foreign minor in an institution, in a child protection structure or in a foster family – Re-examination of final court judgments due to a final decision of the European Court of Human Rights – Harmonization with Law 4624/2019 on the use of information by the Joint Investigation Teams to be applied during the execution of a European Investigation Order – Other provisions, FEK 2024 Issue A' No. 127.

has been a perennial issue.[40] Moreover, the lack of a universal legal definition has been exacerbated by the parallel use of the terms 'refugees', 'asylum/asylum seekers', 'migration', etc. But the latter terms are invariably different in scope and content from what should be properly understood as 'legal migration'. And, importantly, which term should each time be applied to an alien is of fundamental importance because the protection, the rights and the benefits that the Greek State guarantees and affords to them cannot but depend on their proper characterization. However, the lack of definitions is circumvented by considering that any third-country national, to whom one of the residence permits envisaged in Law 5038/2023[41] has been issued, qualifies as a 'migrant', while 'immigration' is the process by virtue of which an alien leaves the country of origin, in the process he becomes an 'immigrant', and while he resides in the host country he is treated as an immigrant pursuant to the domestic legislation in force. It follows that, for the purposes of this monograph, 'immigrant' is an alien ('third-country national' in EU parlance), who has legally entered into the Greek territory and who resides therein on the basis of one of the residence permits that are envisaged in the Immigration Code.[42] Depending on the type of residence permit issued by the competent public authority, a migrant is an alien who offers his remunerated employment to an employer who is based in Greece and the place of performance is also in Greece,[43] or an alien who lives and works as a so-called digital nomad,[44] or, more uniquely, an alien, who has been issued with a residence permit to get acquainted with the life in Greek monasteries and convents (monasticism).[45]

*22.* Article 18 of Law 5038/2023 lays down the common rights that third-country nationals have and enjoy, provided of course that they are and remain in lawful residence. 'Common rights' denotes those rights that are afforded to all migrants irrespective of the type of residence permit they have been issued. Specific types of residence permits may afford additional rights to their holder. On the whole, these rights reflect the protection and privileges that the Greek State is obliged to secure to immigrants and, as the case might be, to members of their families as well. Primarily, these rights emanate from the aforementioned three sources, namely the Constitution and the relevant domestic legislation, from treaties where

40. For example, the United Nations International Convention on the Protection of the Rights of All Migrant Workers and Members of their Families, adopted in 1990, *see infra*, does not give any definition of 'migration', while it defines the term 'migrant worker' as being a person who is engaged in a remunerated activity in a State of which he or she is not a national.
41. The various types of residence permits are laid down in Art. 9 of Law 5038/2023.
42. Note that as it is not explicitly stated in Law 5038/2023 whether refugees are included in this definition, it is the understanding of the author that they are not.
43. *See* Arts 26 and 27 of Act 5038/2023.
44. *See* Art. 68 of Act 5038/2023. Residence permits for the so-called digital nomads were first introduced in the Greek legislation in September 2021 under the aforementioned Law 4825/2021. The idea is to allow nationals coming from non-EU Member States and from non-EEA countries (including Switzerland), to live and work in Greece as entrepreneurs, remote workers, freelancers and, generally, as self-employed people. This category of residence permits is valid for up to two years and, thereafter, they are renewable every two years for an additional period of two years. Presumably, the so-called 3S (it stands for sea, sand, and sun) are enough to lure educated third-country nationals to Greece and make them choose it as their second home.
45. *See* Art. 79 of Act 5038/2023.

Greece is a contracting party (primarily global and regional conventions protecting human rights and fundamental freedoms, conventions adopted under the auspices of the International Labour Organization (ILO), etc.), and from the relevant provisions of EU law. It follows that when a third-country national is issued with a residence permit he immediately enjoys an array of rights and benefits and is also immediately placed under the protection of the law.

*23.* More specifically, Article 18 of Law 5038/2023 stipulates that: (a) the freedom of movement and the freedom of establishment of migrants throughout the Greek territory shall be guaranteed; (b) should third-country nationals have access to the labour market, in other words if they are migrant workers, they shall be insured in the relevant (public) social security institution/organization and shall have the same rights and the same obligations as Greek nationals; (c) if they are detained, they must promptly be informed, in a language that they understand, about the detention centre's rules and regulations as well as about their rights and obligations during detention;[46] (d) under-age third-country nationals, who live in the Greek territory, must attend the compulsory state school programme just like Greek pupils;[47] and (e) third-country nationals, who have graduated from secondary education in Greece, have access to higher education (tertiary level education, Universities, etc.) under the same terms and conditions as Greek students.

*24.* The obligations that migrants must observe and fulfil are laid down in Article 19 of Law 5038/2023. They are mainly of a procedural nature. Thus, migrants must declare to the competent public authorities any change of their residential address, any changes in their personal situation (e.g., change of citizenship, marriage, dissolution/annulment of marriage, birth of children, death of spouse or children when the migrant's residence permit covers them, etc.), and the loss of their official documents (passport, visa, residence permit, etc.).[48] Moreover, migrants must depart from the Greek territory without further notice until the last day of the expiration of their residence permit, unless, before expiration, they have duly applied for its renewal, in which case the temporal validity of the residence permit is extended until the competent public administration authority has reached a decision on its

46. Their communication with the appointed lawyer must be facilitated and the same applies as regards the communication with the diplomatic or consular officials of the State of which they are nationals, which may or may not be the country of origin. This obligation, which relates to the so-called diplomatic protection that a third state may exercise to protect its citizens abroad, derives from the Vienna Convention on Consular Relations, signed on 24 Apr. 1963, entered into force on 19 Mar. 1967, 596 *U.N.T.S.* 291, ratified by Greece under Law 90/1975, FEK 1975 Issue A' 150. The Vienna Convention envisages the right of all foreign nationals, regardless of their migration status, to contact a consular official of the country of origin in case they are arrested, imprisoned, or placed into custody or detention. The obligation of the host country corresponding to this right is to promptly inform migrants of their rights under the Vienna Convention. There are presently 182 contracting states to the Vienna Convention.
47. Schooling in Greece is compulsory for ten years including kindergarten. Pre-primary, primary, secondary, higher and tertiary education as well as undergraduate University studies are provided by the Greek State for free to both Greek nationals and third-country nationals.
48. These declarations have to be made through the electronic services maintained by the Ministry of Migration and Asylum (Integrated Information System 'Migration').

renewal. It follows that, if for whatever reason a migrant has not applied for renewal or his application was rejected, his presence in the Greek territory is not considered to be any longer lawful, unless he can produce another title on the basis of which he continues to be in lawful residence. For example, in theory, an alien with an expired residence permit issued for employment, if during his residence in Greece, he has bought real estate property, he may be able to remain in the country if he were to apply and were granted a residence permit issued to investors (the so-called Gold visa, reference to which has already been made).

*25.* The latter observation leads to the distinction between regular migrants and irregular migrants,[49] especially migrant workers. The employment of irregular residing third-country nationals is strictly prohibited, and severe criminal sanctions are threatened against employers and those taking advantage of their services. This is actually another area of immigration law that is regulated under EU law.[50] The irregular status of a migrant worker does not mean that the employer is not obliged to pay them the wages corresponding to the employment performed. In particular, Article 81 of Law 4052/2012 stipulates that employers must pay them the minimum wage provided by the legislation as well as an amount equal to all contributions and taxes that employers would have paid if they had been legally employed.

*26.* Article 175 Law 5038/2023 stipulates that the policy of social integration not only aims at the adaptation of third-country nationals to Greek society but also that the Greek society recognizes that their equal participation in its economic, social and cultural life will be possible. The general idea is that, during the process of integration into Greek society, migrants will, on the one hand, acquire rights and obligations just like Greek nationals, and, on the other hand, must respect the country's legal order and the fundamental values of the Greek society.[51] Law 5038/2023 further envisages the implementation of a national integration strategy, which will be based on four pillars. *First*, the pre-integration of those foreigners who have applied for international protection. *Second*, the social integration of those who are entitled to international protection. *Third*, the prevention and the effective protection of foreigners from all forms of violence, exploitation and abuse. *Fourth*, the monitoring

49. Generally, *see* M. Ambrosini and M.H.J. Hajer, *Irregular Migration* (Springer, 2023).
50. *See* Arts 79 et seq. of Law 4052/2012, Legislation falling into the competence of the Ministries of Health and Social Solidarity and Labour and Social Security for the implementation of the law 'Approval of the Draft Financial Facility Agreements between the European Financial Stability Facility (EFSF), the Hellenic Republic and the Bank of Greece, the Draft Memorandum of Understanding between the Hellenic Republic, the European Commission and the Bank of Greece and other urgent provisions for the reduction of the public sector debt and saving the national economy' and other provisions, FEK 2012 Issue A' No. 41. Law 4052/2012 transposed into the Greek legal order Directive 2009/52/EC of the European Parliament and of the Council of 18 Jun. 2009 providing for minimum standards on sanctions and measures against employers of illegally staying third-country nationals, O.J. L 168, 30.6.2009, p. 24. Pursuant to Art. 88 of Law 4052/2012, whoever knowingly and systematically employs illegal migrants faces a term of imprisonment of between five months and five years. In addition, administrative sanctions may be inflicted by the competent State authorities. These provisions have been codified in Law 5038/2023. Note that, according to Art. 27(1) of Directive 2009/52, it had to be transposed into domestic law before 20 Jul. 2011.
51. Note that the text of Law 5038/2023 does not contain a general clause stipulating that immigrants must follow and respect the domestic legislation and regulations at all times.

of integration, a responsibility that was bestowed to the Ministry of Migration and Asylum. It is rather interesting that, while Law 5038/2023 talks about a strategy for integration, it makes no reference to the National Integration Strategy, which was adopted in July 2019 by the Ministry of Migration Policy.[52] Or to the National Strategy for the social integration of asylum seekers and international protection of beneficiaries, which was published by the Ministry of Migration and Asylum in January 2022.[53]

*27.* It should also be noted that the new Immigration Code was amended, for the first time, before it had even entered into force and, for the second time, less than a week after it came into force. More specifically, the first amendments were made under Law 5078/2023 (it was promulgated just before Christmas 2023),[54] as follows: Article 190 was of minor importance, namely a linguistic restatement of Article 23 of Law 5038/2023; Article 191 created two new executive positions in the Ministry of Immigration and Asylum, the first being the 'National Coordinator on Returns' and the second the 'National Coordinator against Illegal Trafficking of Migrants'. The persons to hold the respective office are appointed by a joint decision of the Minister of Immigration and Asylum and the Minister of Citizen Protection. For both these positions only active or pensioned senior officers of the Hellenic Police are eligible for selection; Article 193, without making any reference to the Immigration Code, introduced a new type of residence permit to be issued to third-country nationals for employment purposes, subject to certain conditions and requirements, which should be considered to be additional to those which are envisaged in the Immigration Code; and Article 194, which entered into force on the day the Immigration Code came into force and affords to the beneficiaries of temporary international protection the possibility to apply for one of the categories of residence permits that are envisaged in the Immigration Code.

*28.* The second amendment, effected under Law 5100/2024, was of considerable importance and had to do with the conditions for offering to third-country nationals the so-called Gold visas, a type of long-term residence permit granted for investments in real estate.[55] Since then, the Immigration Code was amended under

52. For further information, *see* https://migration.gov.gr/en/migration-policy/integration/politiki-entaxis-se-ethniko-epipedo/. Before the adoption of the 2019 Strategy (it has not been translated in any language), the applicable instrument was the National Strategy for the Integration of Third-Country Nationals, which has been prepared by the Ministry of the Interiors. It was also not available in English and to the best of one's knowledge it was never carried out.

53. Available in English at: https://migration.gov.gr/wp-content/uploads/2022/09/NATIONAL-STRATEGY-FINAL.pdf.

54. Law 5078/2023, Reform of occupational insurance, rationalization of the insurance legislation, pension arrangements, appointment system for and recruitment of teachers in the public employment service, and other provisions, FEK 2023 Issue A' No. 21.

55. As will be explained, the very large number of 'Gold visas' severely disturbed the Greek housing market. In an attempt to resolve this, the government amended the relevant provisions of the Immigration Code, among others, by increasing the minimum amount to be invested in real estate before a third-country national is eligible to apply for a 'Gold visa'.

Law 5130/2024,[56] which brought changes to Article 64 and to Article 65 of Law 5038/2023, as well as under Articles 39–46 of Law 5162/2014, which introduced a new type residence permit for investing in start-up companies (*see infra*).[57]

*29.* To conclude this overview of the Code of Immigration presently in force (Law 5038/2023, as amended), Greece has in place an adequate regulatory framework for the protection of the legal position and, more generally, for safeguarding the rights of regular immigrants. It fully complies with the peremptory rules of public international law and with the various treaties and agreements that the Hellenic Republic has ratified or acceded to. Especially, in areas such as employment, social security, schooling, education, access to the health care system, and others, third-country nationals are treated on an equal basis with Greek nationals and the nationals of the other Member States of the European Union. Moreover, second-generation migrants, who were born in Greece and have lived in the country without interruptions, are entitled, subject to conditions, to apply for Greek citizenship from the day they enrol in the first grade of primary school.[58] What, however, the Greek legal system on immigration lacks is, on the one hand, consistency and codification and, on the other hand, a coherent, consistent, and well-planned national policy for the efficient integration of immigrants and the members of their families benefiting both the Greek State and the migrants themselves.

## III. Administrative Authorities and Judicial Authorities

*30.* As mentioned, for the first time a Ministry responsible for immigration was established in 2016. Three years later, it was dissolved and substituted by the Ministry of Migration and Asylum. Presently, the Ministry is made up of two General Secretariats: the Residence Permits General Secretariat and the General Secretariat of Migration Policy. The former is the competent public authority to issue all types of residence permits; it is also mandated to offer support services to third-country nationals. It is divided into the following three Departments: (a) the Department of Residence Permits of Third-Country Nationals; (b) the Department of Residence Permits for Third-Country Nationals who are Investors; and (c) the Department of Servicing Third-Country Nationals. The General Secretariat of Migration Policy has

56. *See* Arts 48 and 49 of Law 5130/2024, Strengthening of the control system for the Asset Declarations and the Declarations of Financial Interests envisaged in Law 5026/2023 – Placement of a foreign minor in an institution, in a child protection structure or in a foster family – Re-examination of final court judgments due to a final decision of the European Court of Human Rights – Harmonization with Law 4624/2019 on the use of information by the Joint Investigation Teams to be applied during the execution of a European Investigation Order – Other provisions, FEK 2024 Issue A' No. 127.
57. Law 5162/2024, Income support measures, tax incentives for innovation and business transformations and other provisions, FEK 2024 Issue A' No. 198.
58. *See* Law 3284/2004, Ratification of the Code on Hellenic Nationality, FEK 2004 Issue A' No. 217, as presently in force.

as its operational objective the planning and implementation of a national immigration policy, the management of any issue that is related to the legal entry and residence of third-country nationals in Greece, the coordination and supervision of the so-called Decentralized Administrations[59] in matters of immigration, the maintenance of integrity as well as the operation and management of the so-called Single Point of Contact (SPOC).[60] The General Secretariat of Migration Policy is further divided into the following four Departments: (a) the Department of Institutional Operation; (b) the Department of SPOC and Electronic Certification Authority; (c) the Biometric Data Quality Assurance Department; and (d) the Control Department.

*31.* In each of the seven Decentralized Administrations, there is a 'Directorate on Aliens and Migration', which is the competent public authority to handle matters relating to the legal entry of third-country nationals into the Greek territory, relating to legal residence[61] as well as relating to the employment of legally residing third-country nationals. In other words, said Directorate is the public authority that executes and implements the applicable legislation as regards the (legal) entry of aliens as well as the granting, renewing, rejecting, and revoking residence permits.

---

59. The Decentralized Administrations are a relatively new structure in Greek public administration (they were established in 2011). Generally, *see* Council of Europe, Congress of Local and Regional Authorities, 'Local and regional democracy in Greece', 28th Session, Strasbourg, 24–26 Mar. 2015, CG/2015(28)8FINAL, 26 Mar. 2015, at: https://rm.coe.int/local-and-regional-democracy-in-greece-rapporteurs-artur-torres-pereir/168071980e. More specifically, they are independent administrative units responsible for exercising the Greek State's executive and control activities in their areas of responsibility, which include, apart from matters relating to aliens and migration, urban planning, environmental affairs, energy policy, forestry, etc. Essentially, they carry out devolved State powers. The whole of the Greek territory has been divided in seven such Decentralized Administrations, namely Attica; Macedonia and Thrace; Epirus and Western Macedonia; Thessaly and Central Hellas; the Peloponnese, Western Hellas and the Ionian; the Aegean; and Crete. Each Decentralized Administration is made up of several prefectures and has its seat usually in the largest, most populous city in the area covered by it. They enjoy administrative as well as financial autonomy. Each of the seven Decentralized Administrations is headed by a Secretary, who is appointed and dismissed by a decision of the government, in effect they are government appointees. It should be clarified that the Decentralized Administrations are separate entities from the structures of local administration. This follows from Arts 101 and 102 of the Constitution, which provide that the administration of the State shall be organized according to the system of decentralization (Art. 101), hence the Decentralized Administrations, while the administration of local affairs shall belong to the local self-government organizations of the first degree and of the second degree (Art. 102), hence the 332 municipalities that presently operate (local administration of first degree) and the thirteen regions in which the Greek territory has been divided (local administration of second degree). The Regions are the following: Attica, Eastern Macedonia and Thrace, North Aegean, Western Hellas, Western Macedonia, Epirus, Thessaly, Ionian Islands, Central Macedonia, Crete, South Aegean, the Peloponnese, and Central Hellas. Thus, Attica, the Peloponnese and Crete are at the same time Decentralized Administrations and Regions.
60. These are e-government portals that allow service providers to get the information they need and complete administrative procedures online, *see* https://single-market-economy.ec.europa.eu/single-market/services/directive/points-single-contact_en.
61. Note that Art. 3 of Law 5038/2023 defines 'illegal stay' as follows: the presence in Greek territory of a third-country national who does not meet or has ceased to meet the entry requirements, as these are laid down in Art. 6(1) of EU Regulation 2016/399 (the aforementioned 'Schengen Borders Code'), or any other conditions of entry, stay or residence.

The Directorate on Aliens and Migration has its seat in the same city as the respective Decentralized Administration, while at the level of each prefecture, there is a 'Department of Residence Permits' in operation. Since the end of 2022, the most important procedures relating to residence permits are not carried out in person but exclusively electronically.[62] More specifically, the aforementioned General Secretariat of Migration Policy has set up an online platform, which presently facilitates, on the one hand, third-country nationals to submit applications for the initial issuance and renewal of residence permits or for being granted residence permits for exceptional reasons and, on the other hand, employers opportunity to submit electronically applications for inviting seasonal migrant workers to be employed in the agricultural sector.[63] Moreover, the status of the applications lodged by third-country nationals can also be checked electronically by entering their surname and passport number on the relevant webpage of the Ministry of Migration and Asylum.[64]

*32.* As regards the organization and jurisdiction of judicial authorities, in Greece courts of justice are distinguished into three categories: those litigating civil matters, those litigating criminal matters, and those litigating administrative matters. There are correspondingly three codes of procedure regulating the proceedings before them: the Code of Civil Procedure,[65] the Code of Criminal Procedure (CCP),[66] and the Code of Administrative Procedure.[67] Hierarchically speaking, courts of justice are structured as follows: Justices of the Peace; courts of justice of the first instance first-instance (civil[68]/criminal[69]/administrative courts); courts of justice of appeal (civil/criminal/administrative); and Supreme Courts.

*33.* There are three Supreme Courts: (a) *Areios Pagos*, which is competent to hear applications for cassation brought against civil courts of appeal and criminal

62. *See* Decision No. 374365/2021 of the Minister of Migration and Asylum, FEK 2021 Issue B' No. 5242, and Decision No. 674588/2022 of the Minister of Migration and Asylum, FEK 2022 Issue B' No. 5801.
63. For the online facility, *see* https://applications.migration.gov.gr/en/metanasteusi/. Note that all these actions have financed primarily by the EU.
64. *See* https://pf.emigrants.ypes.gr/pf/?lang=en.
65. Presidential Decree 503/1985, Codification of the Code of Civil Procedure, FEK 1985 Issue A' No. 182, as lastly amended by Law 5108/2024, Consolidation of the first degree of jurisdiction, spatial restructuring of the courts of civil and criminal justice and other provisions, FEK 2024 Issue A' No. 65.
66. Law 4620/2019, Ratification of the Code of Criminal Procedure, FEK 2019 Issue A' No. 96, as lastly amended by Law 5108/2024, *ibid.* Generally, *see* I.G. Anagnostopoulos and K.D. Magliveras, *Criminal Law in Greece* (2nd ed., Aan den Rijn: Wolters Kluwer, 2023) 175 et seq.
67. Law 2690/1999, Ratification of the Code of Administrative Procedure and other provisions, FEK 1999 Issue A' No. 45, as lastly amended by Law 4962/2022, Upgrading police training, reforming the framework of organization and operation of the School of Greek Police Officers and other regulations of the Ministry of Citizen Protection, FEK 2022 Issue A' no. 148.
68. *See* Art. 94 of the Constitution.
69. *See* Art. 96 of the Constitution.

courts of appeal; (b) the Council of State, which is competent to hear disputes falling into the ambit of the Greek public administration as well as applications for cassation brought against administrative courts of appeal;[70] and (c) the Hellenic Court of Audit, which functions as the country's supreme financial court and audit institution. There is no Constitutional Court in Greece but, in theory, any court of justice (including the lower ones) is allowed to control the constitutionality of any legislative instrument and to pronounce it unconstitutional. However, a legislative provision that has been declared unconstitutional (even by *Areios Pagos* or the Council of State) does not automatically become null and void and the prevailing view is that the State authorities and organs are not obliged to disapply. Arguably, the consequences of holding a legislative provision unconstitutional are rather a grey area of the Greek legal system. Finally, the question of whether the parliamentarians who voted in favour of the unconstitutional laws/provisions and/or the President of the Hellenic who promulgated them bear any responsibility has not been addressed.

*34.* According to the Greek legal system, the issuance, extension, rejection, etc., of entry visas as well as of residence permits constitute administrative acts (decisions) of the State. The relevant legal term can be translated as 'individual administrative act'/'administrative act of individual concern', in other words, a decision which has been reached by the relevant public authority, has followed the relevant procedure, is in compliance with the appropriate legislation, and is addressed to a specific person. It is of no consequence if the aggrieved person is a Greek national or a third-country national or a stateless person. Access of all persons to the competent courts of justice without discrimination on the grounds of nationality, etc., and without any hindrances (including lack of funds) are principles embedded in the Greek legal order since the country's War of Independence against the Ottoman Empire in the 1820s. Considering that entry visas and residence permits are acts emanating from the public administration, effectively the State, they come within the jurisdiction of the administrative courts of justice. Therefore, actions brought by migrants for annulment of the act revoking a residence permit, or actions alleging that the public administration violated the legislation or breached the relevant procedures, or actions claiming that the competent public authority did not act even though it was under an obligation to do so (actions for omission), and so on, will ordinarily be brought before the administrative Court of First Instance that has territorial jurisdiction (normally the place of the seat of the administrative authority that issued the act/decision complained against).

## §2. The Constitutional Provisions on and the International Legal Instruments Pertaining to Migration Ratified by Greece

*35.* In the Greek legal order, the regulation of the process of migration as well as the legal position of migrants derives, directly or indirectly, from three principal

70. *See* further Art. 95 of the Constitution. The Council of State took its name from the French *Conseil d'état.*

sources, namely: (1) the Constitution, (2) the international legal framework, and (3) the regional legal framework. This is in line with the situation in most other European countries. The first source comprises the Constitution (adopted in 1975),[71] the relevant domestic legislation (primarily, the Code on Immigration) as well as the various legal instruments which have been issued to implement the legislation (presidential decrees and ministerial decisions). The Constitution mentions the words 'alien'/'foreigner' only once. The relevant provision is Article 5(3), which reads: 'It is prohibited to extradite an alien who is prosecuted for his action in favour of freedom.'[72] However, even though in the remainder of Article 5 these words are not mentioned, it is a stark reminder that the Greek legal order treats all foreigners on an equal footing with Greek nationals, with the obvious exception of rights and privileges that emanate from or are associated with citizenship. Thus, Article 5(1) provides that '*Everyone* has the right to freely develop his personality and to participate in the social, economic and political life of the country, provided that he does not violate the rights of others, and he does not violate the Constitution or good morals (*bonos mores*)'. And the second paragraph of Article 5 provides that: '*Whoever* finds himself inside the Greek territory, enjoys the ultimate protection of life, honour and freedom, without any discrimination on the grounds of nationality, race, language, religion or political beliefs. Exceptions are allowed in those instances which are stipulated in international law' (emphasis added).

*36.* The second source comprises all the relevant treaties and conventions, which have been adopted under the auspices of the Organization of the United Nations (UN) as well as of the ILO and which have been ratified by Greece. Greece is a founding Member State of both the UN (1945) and the ILO (1919). Given that presently all sovereign states participate in the UN, and almost all of them are ILO Member States as well, this second source could be said to constitute a globalized or universal legal regime. It is in effect a juridical system that primarily focuses on the protection of human rights and the fundamental freedoms of all people residing in the UN and/or ILO Member State, irrespective of nationality, ethnic origin and other distinguishing characteristics. Therefore, it is a legal regime that, in principle, covers all aliens, including migrants. Indeed, the reasons for which someone has left his country of origin are of no consequence.

*37.* As regards the UN, Greece is a contracting party to all UN human rights treaties (the so-called core treaties),[73] with one notable exception: the International

71. The Constitution of the Hellenic Republic was amended for the fourth time in 2019, FEK 2019 Issue A' No. 211. For an unofficial translation into English, *see* https://www.hellenicparliament.gr/UserFiles/f3c70a23-7696-49db-9148-f24dce6a27c8/THE%20CONSTITUTION%20OF%20GREECE.pdf.

72. *See* further, Art. 1 of Protocol No. 7 to the Convention for the Protection of Human Rights and Fundamental Freedoms, signed on 22 Nov. 1984, entered into force on 1 Nov. 1998, *European Treaty Series* (ETS) No. 117. Greece ratified it under Law 1705/1987, FEK 1987 Issue A' No. 89. *See also infra* discussion on international protection.

73. Greece has also ratified most of the optional Protocols that have been attached to the core treaties. For specific details on the ratifications, declarations and reservations entered by Greece, *see* https://indicators.ohchr.org/.

Convention on the Protection of the Rights of All Migrant Workers and Members of their Families.[74] However, it is not a coincidence that none of the countries participating in the EU and none of the countries of the so-called Western world has become a contracting party to it or has signed it for that matter. The reason is that, as will be explained *infra*, the EU has its own binding legal system regulating intra-EU migration and over the years has adopted its own rules to regulate also in a binding fashion the access of aliens to its Member States. Finally, as regards the immigration-related treaties, which have been negotiated and concluded under the auspices of the ILO, Greece has ratified several of them.[75]

*38.* The third source comprises ratified treaties and other binding legal instruments relating to migration that have been adopted by the regional international organizations in which Greece is a Member State. More specifically, as has been mentioned, Greece is a Member State of the Council of Europe, and Greece further acceded on 1 January 1981 to the European Economic Community (now, the EU). As regards the Council of Europe, several relevant treaties have been adopted under its auspices over the years making it the only regional international organization with such extensive regulatory activities in the area of migration and asylum. Greece has become a contracting party to most of them[76] and has signed but not ratified or has not signed at all four of them.[77]

---

74. It was adopted by the UN General Assembly on 18 Dec. 1990, entered into force on 1 Jul. 2003, 2220 *U.N.T.S.* 3. There are presently fifty-nine contracting parties.
75. Greece is a contracting party to the following ILO treaties (in chronological order of adoption): (a) the Convention concerning Freedom of Association and Protection of the Right to Organise, which was adopted in 1950 (ILO Convention No. 87), ratified under Legislative Decree 4204/1961, FEK 1961 Issue A' No. 174; (b) the Convention concerning the Application of the Principles of the Right to Organise and to Bargain Collectively, 1949 (ILO Convention No. 98), ratified under Legislative Decree 4205/1961, FEK 1961 Issue A' No. 174; (c) the Equal Remuneration Convention, 1951 (ILO Convention No. 100), ratified under Law 46/1975, FEK 1975 Issue A' No. 105; and (d) the Convention concerning Discrimination in Respect of Employment and Occupation, 1958 (ILO Convention No. 111), ratified under Law 1424/1984, FEK 1984 Issue A' No. 29. Greece is *not* a contracting party to the Migration for Employment Convention (Revised), 1949 (ILO Convention No. 97), to the Migrant Workers (Supplementary Provisions) Convention, 1975 (ILO Convention No. 143), and to the Domestic Workers Convention, 2011 (ILO Convention No. 189).
76. Greece is a contracting party to the following: (a) the European Convention on Establishment (ETS No. 19), which was adopted in 1955 (ratified in 1965), 529 *U.N.T.S.* 142; (b) the European Agreement on Regulations governing the Movement of Persons between Member States of the Council of Europe (ETS No. 25) adopted in 1957 (ratified under Law 4077/1960, FEK 1960 Issue A' No. 106), 1562 *U.N.T.S.* 327; (c) the European Social Charter (ETS No. 35) adopted in 1961 (ratified under Law 1426/1984, FEK 1984 Issue A' No. 32), 529 *U.N.T.S.* 89, the Additional Protocol to the European Social Charter (ETS No. 128) adopted in 1988 as well as the Additional Protocol to the European Social Charter Providing for a System of Collective Complaints (ETS No. 158) adopted in 1995 (ratified under Law 2595/1998, FEK 1998 Issue A' No. 63); and (d) the Revised European Social Charter (ETS No. 163) adopted in 1996 (ratified under Law 4359/2016, FEK 2016 Issue A' No. 5). For further information on these treaties, *see* the Treaty Office of the Council of Europe at: https://www.coe.int/en/web/conventions/full-list.
77. Namely, the European Convention on the Legal Status of Migrant Workers (ETS No. 93) adopted in 1977, 1496 *U.N.T.S.* 3; the Convention on the Participation of Foreigners in Public Life at Local Level (ETS No. 144) adopted in 1992; the European Agreement on the Abolition of Visas for Refugees (ETS No. 31) adopted in 1959, 376 *U.N.T.S.* 85; and the European Agreement on Transfer of Responsibility for Refugees (ETS No. 107) adopted in 1980, 1249 *U.N.T.S.* 383.

*39.* As regards the legal system of the EU (the EU law), it is important to note that it has its own binding rules pertaining to the nationals (and members of their families) of any of the twenty-seven Member States emigrating to any other Member State in pursuance of the so-called free movement of persons. This is a cornerstone of the Common Market (also known as the 'EU Internal Market') that has existed in the EU for many decades now. It mostly has to do with the fact that the EU belongs to the category of international organizations referred to as 'regional economic integration organisations' (REIOs). Thus, the free movement of persons is one of the very fundamental principles of EU law. It is enshrined in Article 3(2) of the Treaty on European Union (TEU), in Article 21 of the Treaty on the Functioning of the European Union (TFEU) as well as in Article 45 of the EU Charter of Fundamental Rights.[78]

*40.* It is of some importance to understand that these sources interact with each other, in the sense that the Constitution as well as the domestic legislation on immigration must always be in conformity with and never breach ratified treaties and other binding instruments that have been adopted by the international organizations in which Greece is a Member State. In the case of the EU, these would be the so-called Founding Treaties, namely the TEU and the TFEU, the Charter of Fundamental Freedoms, as well as the relevant secondary legislation, which invariably takes the form of regulations and directives. However, the right of the nationals of EU Member States to move freely from one Member State to the other[79] is not unconditional and must always be exercised in accordance with the conditions and restrictions placed by EU law.[80]

*41.* The equal treatment between Greek nationals and aliens, including migrants, or, to put it otherwise, the obligation of the Greek State to ensure the equal treatment of the whole population, derives, *inter alia*, from the prohibition of discrimination on the grounds of nationality, is stipulated in the Greek Constitution.[81] At the same time, this is one of the cornerstones of international human rights law, whose rules are to a large extent applicable to the process of migration and, more generally, to the protection of the rights of aliens. The prohibition of discrimination as a peremptory rule of human rights law does not only cover the question of nationality but also extends to many other features and characteristics of the human being, including sex, race, colour, language, religion, wealth, political opinion, etc.[82]

---

78. All ratified under Law 3671/2008, Ratification of the Treaty on European Union, the Treaty on the Functioning of the European Union, and certain other relevant acts, FEK 2008 Issue A' No. 129.
79. *See* European Commission, *Commission Notice: Guidance on the Right of Free Movement of EU Citizens and Their Families*, C/2023/8500, published on 22 Dec. 2023, at: https://eur-lex.europa.eu/eli/C/2023/1392/oj.
80. *See* further, Titles IV and V TFEU and discussion *infra*.
81. *See also* Art. 2(1) of the Constitution: 'Respect and protection of the value of the human being constitute the primary obligations of the State'.
82. *See*, *inter alia*, Art. 2 of the Universal Declaration of Human Rights (UDHR), which was adopted and proclaimed by UN General Assembly as Resolution 217 A (III) of 10 Dec. 1948, and Art. 2(1) of the International Covenant on Civil and Political Rights (ICCPR), adopted on 16 Dec. 1966 under UN General Assembly Resolution 2200 A (XXI), entered into force on 23 Mar. 1976, 999 *UNTS* 171, ratified by Law 2462/1997, FEK 1997 Issue A' No. 25. Note that in the ECHR, the prohibition

Finally, the EU has issued common rules on the basis of which Member States must ensure the principle of equal treatment at work. These rules, which could very well be to the benefit of third-country nationals as well,[83] were incorporated into the Greek legal order by virtue of Law 4443/2016.[84] Two aspects of Law 4443/2026 should be mentioned. First, it envisages the imposition of fines and other sanctions for violating the principle of equal treatment at work. Second, it provides that those affected must be offered judicial protection, that the burden of proof for the alleged violation shall be reversed and that third-country nationals are protected from countermeasures taken against them. Arguably, in the case of migration, the prohibition of discrimination operates on two different levels. The first level is the prohibition of discrimination between Greek nationals on the one hand and immigrants on the other hand. Here, as will later be explained, the legislation does not allow, for example, in the sphere of (state) social security that Greek nationals have a more comprehensive medical insurance compared to migrant workers. The second level is the prohibition of discrimination among migrants themselves, where, it should be accepted, that discrimination is allowed if it is justified based on the international obligations that Greece has assumed or if the EU allows it. To offer an example, reference will be made to Article 65 of the current Immigration Code (Law 5038/2023), which is titled 'Rights – Equal treatment of third-country nationals, who are seasonal workers'. As will be explained in more detail *infra*, Article 65 transposed into Greek law Articles 22 and 23 of the EU Directive regulating the presence and the employment of seasonal migrant workers in the territory of all Member

---

of discrimination was originally laid down in Art. 14. Later, its content was augmented under Art. 1 of Protocol No. 12 to the ECHR, adopted on 4 Nov. 2000, entered into force on 1 Apr. 2005 (*ETS* No. 177), Greece signed it on the day it was adopted but has not yet ratified it. Protocol No. 12 introduced a more general prohibition of discrimination in the enjoyment of any right set forth by law, *see* European Court of Human Rights, *Guide on Article 14 of the European Convention on Human Rights and on Article 1 of Protocol No. 12 to the Convention: Prohibition of Discrimination*, Updated on 31 Aug. 2024, at: https://ks.echr.coe.int/documents/d/echr-ks/guide_art_14_art_1_protocol_12_eng.

83. *See* Council Directive 2000/43/EC of 29 Jun. 2000 implementing the principle of equal treatment between persons irrespective of racial or ethnic origin, O.J. L 180, 19.7.2000, p. 22; Council Directive 2000/78/EC of 27 Nov. 2000 establishing a general framework for equal treatment in employment and occupation, O.J. L 303, 2.12.2000, p. 16. Note that the equal treatment as well as the prohibition of discrimination applies in principle to nationals of third countries as well. However, it does not cover differences of treatment that are based on nationality, and it is without prejudice to those provisions that govern the entry and residence of third-country nationals as well as their access to employment and occupation.

84. *See* Law 4443/2016, (i) Incorporation of Directive 2000/43/EC on the implementation of the principle of equal treatment of persons regardless of racial or ethnic origin, of Directive 2000/78/EC on the establishment of a general framework for equal treatment in employment and work, and of Directive 2014/54/EU on measures that facilitate the exercise of workers' rights in the context of the free movement of workers; (ii) Taking the necessary measures to comply with Arts 22, 23, 30, 31(1), 32 and 34 of Regulation 596/2014 on market abuse and the repeal of Directive 2003/6/EC of the European Parliament and of the Council and of Commission Directives 2003/124/EC, 2003/125 EC and 2004/72/EC and incorporation of Directive 2014/57/EU on criminal sanctions for market abuse and Implementing Directive 2015/2392; (iii) Incorporation of Directive 2014/62 on the protection of the euro and other currencies against counterfeiting by criminal law, and replacing Council Framework Decision 2000/383/JHA, and (iv) Establishment of a National Mechanism to Investigate Incidents of Arbitrariness by the security forces and the employees of detention centres, and other provisions, FEK 2016 Issue A' No. 232.

States.[85] And while Article 65 sets out the areas where seasonal migrant workers shall enjoy equal treatment with Greek nationals, there is no reference to immigrants having equal treatment among them. Equally, Article 82 of Law 5038/2023, which provides that those migrant workers, who are not seasonally employed, shall enjoy equal treatment with Greek nationals, does not mention the equal treatment of migrant workers among them.[86]

*42.* To expand on the aforementioned principal sources regarding the regulation of immigration in Greece, it should be emphasized that the obligations and duties that are binding vis-à-vis the process of migration derive, in general, from the fact that Greece: (a) participates in several international organizations that are active in the area of migration; and (b) has ratified numerous relevant treaties and conventions, including bilateral agreements. To put it otherwise, while the general principle of international law is that a state may regulate all issues pertaining to immigration as it thinks fit,[87] Greece's membership in international organizations and/or participation in bilateral and multilateral agreements has curtailed its (absolute) right as a (sovereign) state to promulgate whatever legislation it deems appropriate and to pursue whatever policy it favours in the area of immigration.

*43.* This argument is best illustrated by looking into how Greek law has had to be adapted on account of the country's membership in the EU. More specifically, given that the EU has developed its own legal system and has its own unique rules, norms and procedures, as a Member State, Greece must follow the so-called *EU acqui*, which ranks higher than ordinary domestic law and, in cases of conflict, prevails.[88] As already explained, the right to free movement of persons ensures that the nationals of all Member States have an unhindered right to move freely, in other words, to emigrate and to immigrate to all other Member States.[89] This is a right that applies exclusively to those who are nationals of one of the EU Member States; in principle, no citizen of a third state can have this right expressly conferred upon him. It follows that those individuals, who have the nationality of an EU Member State and, by having exercised this right, have emigrated to Greece, enjoy more privileges compared to those immigrants, who are nationals of a non-Member State (third-country nationals).

---

85. Namely, Directive 2014/36/EU of the European Parliament and of the Council of 26 Feb. 2014 on the conditions of entry and stay of third-country nationals for the purpose of employment as seasonal workers, O.J. L 94, 28.3.2014, p. 375.
86. As is later explained, Art. 82 of Law 5038/2023 partly adapted Greek legislation to the terms of EU Directive 2011/98, which contains a common set of rights for third country workers who are legally residing in a Member State.
87. Generally, *see* S. Song, 'Why Does the State Have the Right to Control Immigration?' in J. Knight (ed.), *Immigration, Emigration, and Migration: Nomos LVII* (2017), 3–50. International Organization for Migration/Migration Policy and Research Programme, *International Legal Norms and Migration: An Analysis* (International Dialogue on Migration no. 3, 2002), 15–25.
88. This is the principle of the primacy of EU law over the domestic law of all Member States.
89. Note that under Art. 9 TEU and Art. 20 TFEU, every person who holds the nationality of a Member State is at the same time a citizen of the European Union, hence the term 'EU citizen'.

*44.* It further follows that the latter category of persons may not complain that they have been discriminated against on the grounds of nationality. It should also be explained that nationals of one Member State moving to another for the purpose of employment (effectively, they are 'migrant workers') must enjoy equal treatment with the nationals of other Member States as regards access to employment, working conditions, social benefits, tax advantages, access to education and vocational training, and so on.[90] Moreover, EU law that Member States have the discretion to allow third-country nationals, who lawfully live and work in the Member States, to have the same or comparable rights and benefits as the Member States' nationals. At the same time, an EU Member State could conclude with a third state a bilateral immigration agreement and confer to that third state's nationals the rights, benefits and advantages that are enjoyed by EU citizens, which, effectively, will be the same as those enjoyed by its own nationals.[91] Note nevertheless that an EU Member State cannot give workers from a third country more rights or more benefits compared to those offered to EU citizens because this would have led to giving them more rights or benefits compared to its own nationals. As regards the equal or unequal treatment of migrant workers, reference will be made to the Agreement which was concluded in November 2022 between Egypt and Greece regarding the seasonal employment of Egyptian nationals in the agricultural sector in Greece.[92] During their stay and employment in Greece, the emigrated nationals of Egypt may have the same privileges, compared to the citizens of another third country who can also be seasonally employed in Greece. One such third country is Bangladesh: in February 2022, a bilateral Agreement was concluded that also envisages and regulates the seasonal employment of Bangladeshi nationals in Greece.[93] Consequently, a seasonal migrant worker from Egypt should not be able to complain that he/she has fewer privileges compared to migrants from Bangladesh and vice versa.

---

90. *See* further, Directive 2014/54/EU of the European Parliament and of the Council of 16 Apr. 2014 on measures facilitating the exercise of rights conferred on workers in the context of freedom of movement for workers, O.J. L 128, 30.4.2014, p. 8, and European Commission, Report to the European Parliament, the Council and the European Economic and Social Committee on the implementation of Directive 2014/54/EU of the European Parliament and of the Council of 16 Apr. 2014 on measures facilitating the exercise of rights conferred on workers in the context of freedom of movement for workers, COM(2018)789 final, 4 Dec. 2018. Generally, *see* European Commission, *Annual Report on Intra-EU Labour Mobility 2022* (Luxembourg: Publications Office of the European Union, 2023); and *Annual Report on Intra-EU Labour Mobility 2023* (Luxembourg: Publications Office of the European Union, 2024).
91. On Greece's bilateral Agreements relating to migration, *see* K. Magliveras, 'The National Dimension of Legal Bilateralism in Migration: The Case of Greece' in F. Ippolito, F. Casolari and G. Borzoni (eds), *Bilateral Relations in the Mediterranean: Prospects for Migration Issues* (Cheltenham: Edward Elgar Publishing, 2020) 24–47.
92. Agreement between the Government of the Hellenic Republic and the Government of the Arab Republic of Egypt on the Employment of Seasonal workers in the Agricultural Sector, signed in Cairo on 22 Nov. 2022, ratified by Greece under Law 5009/2023, FEK 2023 Issue A' No. 7. The Agreement falls into the ambit of the aforementioned EU Directive 2014/36 on the conditions for entry and stay of seasonal migrant workers.
93. Memorandum of Understanding between the Government of the Hellenic Republic and the Government of the People's Republic of Bangladesh on Migration and Mobility, signed in Dhaka on 9 Feb. 2022, ratified by Greece under Law 4959/2022, FEK 2022 Issue A' No. 144.

*45.* Finally, it should be noted that in the late 1990s and the 2000s the EU together with its Member States concluded with several third countries of the wider Mediterranean region the so-called Euro-Mediterranean Association Agreements. In some of these Agreements, which to the best of one's knowledge are still valid, the question of migration has been addressed and regulated, albeit with different intensity.[94] More recently, the EU has concluded bilateral agreements and accords with countries in North Africa, including Tunisia[95] and Egypt.[96] The question of migration is one of the main themes of these accords.[97] However, there is a main difference between these accords and the Euro-Mediterranean Association Agreements, namely that the former are primarily concerned with curtailing irregular migration.

*46.* Further, the fact that the regulation of migration into the Member States is a matter of EU law also means that the behaviour of the Member States may be reviewed and scrutinized by the EU. For example, when foreigners submit allegations of fundamental rights violations at the borders of Member States, it is the duty of the latter to carry out effective investigations into the allegations This duty derives from Article 19 TEU, which stipulates that all Member States provide remedies to ensure effective legal protection in the fields covered by EU law. When the EU finds that a Member State is not investigating allegations of fundamental rights during border management, it may decide that it has to act to close the gap. Thus, in 2022, it was recommended that Greece should strengthen the fundamental rights component of its national border management governance structure and, moreover, that it should carry out thorough and prompt investigations of reported serious allegations of ill-treatment of foreigners.[98]

*47.* As Greece participates in other international organizations as well, in reality, there are several bodies and institutions which, directly or indirectly, are in a position to supervise the application, respect and effective enforcement of human rights

94. *See* K. Magliveras, 'Protecting the Rights of Migrant Workers in the Euro-Mediterranean Partnership' 9 *Mediterranean Politics* (2004) (Special Issue on Economic and Social Rights in the Euro-Mediterranean Partnership) 459–488.
95. *See* Memorandum of Understanding on a strategic and global partnership between the European Union and Tunisia, signed in Tunis, Tunisia, on 16 Jul. 2023, at: https://ec.europa.eu/commission/presscorner/detail/en/ip_23_3887.
96. *See* Joint Declaration on the Strategic and Comprehensive Partnership between the Arab Republic of Egypt and the European Union, issued in Cairo, Egypt, on 17 Mar. 2024, at: https://neighbourhood-enlargement.ec.europa.eu/news/joint-declaration-strategic-and-comprehensive-partnership-between-arab-republic-egypt-and-european-2024-03-17_en.
97. Generally, *see* European Commission, Communication from the Commission to the European Parliament, the European Council and the Council, *Striking a balance on migration: an approach that is both fair and firm*, Brussels, 12 Mar. 2024, COM(2024) 126 final.
98. *See* Council of the European Union, Council implementing decision setting out a recommendation on addressing the deficiencies identified in the 2021 evaluation of Greece on the application of the Schengen *acquis* in the field of management of the external borders, 8184/22, Brussels, 12 Apr. 2022, Recommendations 2 and 24, at: https://data.consilium.europa.eu/doc/document/ST-8184-2022-INIT/en/pdf.

norms. Bodies include: the EU Agency for Fundamental Rights (FRA),[99] the European Parliament, the Office of the United Nations High Commissioner for Human Rights, the Office of the United Nations High Commissioner for Refugees, the treaty bodies that operate in the context of the UN core human rights treaties, the Council of Europe's Parliamentary Assembly (PACE),[100] the European Committee for the Prevention of Torture (CPT) and Inhuman or Degrading Treatment or Punishment , and, of course, the ECtHR and the European Court of Justice.[101]

## §3. Statistical Information

*48.* The population in Greece has been in decline for several decades now due to a combination of reasons, which include the mass emigration of Greek nationals,[102] especially during the sovereign debt crisis of the 2010s, a continuously declining birth rate[103] and the repatriation of migrant workers to their countries of origin. Since 2011, the positive balance between births and deaths has been (possibly irreversibly) changed to a negative balance. Thus, in 2019 there were 86,440 births and 119,446 deaths, in 2021 the births had gone down to 85,303, while deaths went up to 143,329, a figure that was admittedly due to the deaths caused by the COVID pandemic. The same could be said about the number of deaths during the year 2022 (140.342 deaths). The number of deaths during 2023 went down to 127.581, which is still higher than the figure for 2019. Finally, during the year 2023, the number of births was only 73,000, the lowest figure in living memory, and 3,000 fewer births compared to the year 2022.

*49.* According to the results of the 2021 population census, the total 'legal population' was 9.7 million (according to the 2011 census it was 9.9 million), while the 'permanent population' stood at 10.4 million against 10.8 million in 2011.[104]

---

99. *See* FRA, 'Guidance on Investigating Alleged Ill-Treatment at Borders', 30 Jul. 2024, at: https://fra.europa.eu/en/publication/2024/guidance-investigating-alleged-ill-treatment-borders.

100. *See*, in particular, the work of the Committee on Migration, Refugees and Displaced Persons, and PACE Resolution 1509 (2006), 'Human Rights of Irregular Migrants', 27 Jun. 2006; and specifically for Greece, PACE Recommendation 2155 (2019), 'The Situation of Migrants and Refugees on the Greek Islands: More Needs to Be Done', 11 Apr. 2019.

101. Note that, as of 1 Jan. 2024, there were thirty one pending cases before the Court which involved alleged ill-treatment of foreigners at the EU's external borders, nine of which were directed against the Hellenic Republic.

102. Generally, *see* C. Kasimis, 'Greece, Migration 1830s to Present' in I. Ness (ed.), *The Encyclopedia of Global Human Migration* (Wiley Online Library, 2013) at: https://doi.org/10.1002/9781444351071.wbeghm259.

103. The fertility rate in Greece is believed to be below the rate of 1.4 which is the minimum to avoid a reclining population. The birth rate for the year 2023 was estimated at 6,930 births per 1,000 people, a 2.5% decline compared to the year 2022, while the birth rate in 2020 was 7,475 births per 1,000 people, a 2.3% decline compared to 2019. As comparison, the fertility rate in 1960 was 2.2, in 1974 it had gone up to 2.4, in 1984 it fell to 1.8, and in 2000 it stood at 1.3. Generally, *see* The World Bank Data, *Fertility-Rated: Greece*, at: https://data.worldbank.org/indicator/SP.DYN.TFRT.IN?locations=GR.

104. The competent state authority, the Hellenic Statistical Authority, has still not uploaded the results of the 2021 census on its English website https://www.statistics.gr/en/2021-census-pop-hous.

According to the Hellenic Statistical Authority, the term 'legal population' means the number of Greek nationals, who were permanently residing in the country and were censured.[105] The term 'permanent population' means the population residing in Greece, both Greek nationals and aliens, whether regularly or irregularly residing in the country. Pursuant to recent data released by the Ministry of Immigration and Asylum, at the end of February 2023 there were roughly 749,000 legal migrants living in Greece, a decline of 6,000 compared to August 2022. Thirty per cent were EU nationals as well as persons of Greek descent who were born in a third state of which they are nationals,[106] 62% were third-country nationals, and the remaining 8% were persons entitled to international protection. As regards third-country nationals, the three largest countries of origin were Albania (60%), China (5%) and Georgia (4.3%). Finally, at the end of February 2023, there were almost 12,000 residence permits in force for investment activities, of which 63% were issued to Chinese nationals and 4.6% to nationals of Lebanon.

*50.* More specifically, according to the 2021 and 2011 population censuses, the resident population by groups of citizenship from the principal geographical regions of the world and the percentage change are as follows (excluding Greek nationality; figures have been rounded up to the nearest zero or five):[107]

- EU countries: 116,670 persons under the 2021 census versus 183,975 persons under the 2011 census[108] (minus 36.5%).
- European countries outside the EU (including Great Britain and Turkey): 439,250 versus 550,550 (minus 20%).
- Countries of Africa: 33,470 versus 25,850 (plus 29.5%).
- Countries of the Caribbean, South or Central America: 3,565 versus 2,563 (plus 39%).
- Countries of North America: 5,610 versus 7,250 (minus 23%).
- Countries of Asia: 158,530 versus 133,115 (plus 19%).
- Countries of Oceania: 1,495 versus 1,994 (minus 25%).

---

However, every two months an e-publication titled 'The Living Conditions in Greece' appears, which offers updated information on changes in the Greek population, the Greek labour market, etc.; they are available at: https://www.statistics.gr/en/living-conditions-in-greece. For more general information, there is also the quarterly publication 'Greece in figures', at: https://www.statistics.gr.

105. Censured means the number of people who were recorded during the duration of the census.

106. These are the so-called omogeneis (literally translated 'as being of the same race'), people who have come to live permanently in Greece principally from Albania, Turkey, countries of the former Soviet Union, North America, etc., and are able to show that they have Hellenic lineage. They are issued with a special identity card and may gain Greek citizenship pursuant to Art. 23 of the aforementioned Law 3838/2010 or, otherwise, pursuant to Art. 7(8) of the aforementioned Law 3284/2004 on the Greek Nationality Code. 'Omogenois' should be distinguished from Greek nationals, who have left the country to reside permanently (or at least more than 181 days per calendar year) in another country, whether in the EU or in a non-EU state. The word 'omogeneis' has been translated as 'repatriated Greeks'. However, as it might not always be an accurate translation, it is avoided in the present monograph.

107. *See* Hellenic Statistical Authority, *Living Conditions in Greece*, 2 May 2024, 15.

108. A census is *a count for official purposes*, especially one to count the number of people living in a country and to obtain information such as age, sex, race, etc.

*51.* Data published by Frontex in December 2023 showed that during the first eleven months of 2023, the Central Mediterranean (i.e., the route from Algeria, Egypt, Libya and Tunisia to Italy and Malta) remained the busiest migratory route with more than 152,200 irregular crossings reported, the highest total on this route since the year 2016. And, as regards the first eight months of 2024, Frontex data showed that the number of irregular border crossings into the EU fell by 39% to 139,847 persons. And while the largest decreases in irregular border crossings were once more recorded on the Western Balkans and Central Mediterranean routes, the Eastern Mediterranean route saw increased migratory pressure from Turkey with smugglers increasingly using speedboats to reach the Greek islands in the Aegean Sea. During the period January–August 2024, the East Mediterranean route recorded a 39% increase to 37,163 persons with the top three nationalities of migrants coming from Syria, Afghanistan and Egypt.

# Part I. Border Control and Entry

## Chapter 1. Organization, Framework and Third-Country Nationals in Transit

*52.* Regarding terminology, it should be noted that Law 5038/2023 uses the following terms, which in ordinary language might have the same or a similar meaning but in Article 1 of the Immigration Code, they have been defined as follows: (a) 'alien or foreigner' is the natural person who does not possess Greek citizenship or who is stateless; (b) 'third-country national' is the natural person who does not possess Greek citizenship or the citizenship of another EU Member State in the meaning of Article 20(1) of the TFEU;[109] (c) 'stateless person' is the natural person who fulfils the conditions laid down in the New York Convention on the Status of Stateless Persons (1954);[110] and (d) 'citizen of the Union' is any person who has the citizenship of a Member State of the European Union.

*53.* According to Article 5(2) of Law 5038/2023, the control of the persons who enter or leave the Greek territory is the responsibility of the Ministry of Citizen Protection (formerly, the Ministry of Public Order). It is carried out by the competent police authority, which is the Hellenic Police.[111] The meaning of this provision is

109. It reads: 'Citizenship of the Union is hereby established. Every person holding the nationality of a Member State shall be a citizen of the Union. Citizenship of the Union shall be additional to and not replace national citizenship.'

110. The Convention was signed on 28 Sep. 1954, entered into force on 6 Jun. 1960, 360 *UNTS* 117. Greece ratified it under Law 139/1975, FEK 1975, Issue A' No. 176. According to Art. 1(1) of the Convention, the term 'stateless person' means a person who is not considered a national by any State under the operation of its law. The Convention does not contain a definition of the term 'State'.

111. In its present structure, the Hellenic Police ('Elliniki Astynomia') was established in 1984, when the so-called Urban Police Forces ('Astynomia Poleon', it was responsible for policing in the capital city Athens and other large cities) merged with the Gendarmerie ('Hellenic Gendarmerie', previously named 'Royal Gendarmerie', it responsible for policing in towns, villages and in the countryside) pursuant to Law 1481/1984, FEK 1984 Issue A' No. 152. The Hellenic Police is a law enforcement agency regulated under Law 2800/2000, Restructuring of the Ministry of Public Order, establishment of the Hellenic Police Headquarters and other provisions, FEK 2000 Issue A' No. 41, as presently in force. Its mission is to ensure peace and public order as well as the unhindered social development of citizens (this relates to general policing and traffic safety duties), the prevention and avoidance of crime as well as the protection the Greek State and the democratic form of government as laid down in the Constitution (this relates to the implementation of a policy of public and state security). Greece has been a member of Interpol since 7 Sep. 1923. The Hellenic Police has participated in Europol since the beginning of its operation, *see* Regulation (EU) 2016/794 of the

that both Greek nationals and aliens are controlled by the Hellenic Police when they enter or when they leave the country. It should be noted that Greece is a contracting party to the Schengen Agreement.[112] Since the year 2000, border controls between Greece and the other EU Member States that participate in the so-called Schengen area have been lifted.[113]

*54.* Presently, there is a common regulatory framework that applies to the Schengen area, the Schengen Borders Code.[114] This framework primarily comprises the following two elements. The first is the institution that has been established for the effective control of the Member States' external borders, namely the European Border and Coast Guard Agency (Frontex).[115] The second is an information-sharing system for security and border management, known as the Schengen Information System (SIS).[116]

*55.* It should be noted that EU Member States, under Articles 25 et seq. of the Schengen Borders Code, have the right to temporarily reintroduce border control at the internal borders (essentially, the Schengen Area) if there are serious threats to public policy or their internal security. However, this must be applied only as a last

---

European Parliament and of the Council of 11 May 2016 on the European Union Agency for Law Enforcement Cooperation (Europol) and replacing and repealing Council Decisions 2009/371/JHA, 2009/934/JHA, 2009/935/JHA, 2009/936/JHA and 2009/968/JHA, O.J. L 135, 24.5.2016, p. 53.

112. *See* Agreement between the Governments of the States of the Benelux Economic Union, the Federal Republic of Germany and the French Republic on the gradual abolition of checks at their common borders, signed on 14 Jun. 1985, O.J. L 239, 22.9.2000, p. 13; and Convention Implementing the Schengen Agreement, signed on 19 Jun. 1990, O.J. L 239, 22.9.2000, p. 19. Greece signed an Agreement on accession to both these treaties in Madrid, Spain, on 6 Nov. 1992, which was ratified rather belatedly under Law 2514/1997, FEK 1997 Issue A' No. 140.

113. The Schengen area started in 1985 as an intergovernmental project between five EU countries (France, Germany, Belgium, the Netherlands and Luxembourg) and has gradually become the largest free travel area in the world in which even non-EU Member States are participants (the so-called Schengen-associated countries). For further information, *see* European Council/Council of the European Union, 'The Schengen area explained' (last review 25 Feb. 2025), available at: https://www.consilium.europa.eu/en/policies/schengen-area/.

114. Regulation (EU) 2016/399 of the European Parliament and of the Council of 9 Mar. 2016 on a Union Code on the rules governing the movement of persons across borders (Schengen Borders Code) (codification), O.J. L 77, 23.3.2016, p. 1.

115. It has its seat in Warsaw, Poland, *see* Regulation (EU) 2019/1896 of 13 Nov. 2019 on the European Border and Coast Guard, O.J. L 295, 14.11.2019, p. 1. It was previously known as the European Agency for the Management of Operational Cooperation at the External Borders of the Member States of the European Union (Frontex), *see* Council Regulation (EC) 2007/2004 of 26 Oct. 2004 establishing a European Agency for the Management of Operational Cooperation at the External Borders of the Member States of the European Union, O.J. L 349, 25.11.2004, p. 1, which had been in operation since 1 Oct. 2005.

116. *See* Regulation (EU) 2018/1861 of the European Parliament and of the Council of 28 Nov. 2018 on the establishment, operation and use of the Schengen Information System (SIS) in the field of border checks, and amending the Convention implementing the Schengen Agreement, and amending and repealing Regulation (EC) No. 1987/2006, O.J. L 312, 7.12.2018, p. 14. It was last amended by Regulation (EU) 2021/1152 of the European Parliament and of the Council of 7 Jul. 2021 amending Regulations (EC) No. 767/2008, (EU) 2017/2226, (EU) 2018/1240, (EU) 2018/1860, (EU) 2018/1861 and (EU) 2019/817 as regards the establishment of the conditions for accessing other EU information systems for the purposes of the European Travel Information and Authorization System, O.J. L 249, 14.7.2021, p. 15.

resort measure, there must be exceptional situations, and the principle of proportionality must always be respected. At the time of writing, the right to reintroduce border controls has been exercised extensively by certain EU Member States; however, Greece has never reintroduced border controls.[117]

*56.* Pursuant to Article 5(1) of Law 5038/2023, persons are permitted to enter the Greek territory and to leave it only from the official border crossing points (these are laid down in the legislation). The surveillance of these crossing points, and more generally of Greece's land and sea borders, is carried out by the police authorities and/or by the coastal guard authorities.[118] Considering that Greece's external borders are part of the Schengen area, their surveillance may be jointly undertaken with Frontex when exceptional situations are present that have a significant impact on EU border security. This happened previously in 2015: the regular joint operation EPN Poseidon Sea 2015 was replaced by the Poseidon Rapid Intervention following a request from Greece to be supported in handling the unprecedented number of migrants landing on its islands in the Aegean Sea.[119]

*57.* The provisions of Law 5038/2023 do not apply to those foreigners who are in the transit zone of a Greek airport or seaport for the purpose of continuing their journey to another third country with the same or with another aircraft or sea vessel. Therefore, for the application of the Immigration Code, being in transit does not constitute entry of a citizen of a third country in the Greek territory. However, an Airport Transit Visa (ATV) might be required; considering that in the EU, there is a Visa Code common to all Member States, each time the applicable EU legislation will set out in which instances an ATV will be required.[120] Finally, Article 5(5) of the law 5038/2023 provides that the Greek control authorities have the right to order a third-country national in transit to leave immediately the Greek territory if they find that he does not meet the conditions for entry into the (single) Schengen area according to the aforementioned Schengen Borders Code.

---

117. *See* European Commission, Migration and Home Affairs, 'Temporary Reintroduction of Border Control', online available at: https://home-affairs.ec.europa.eu/policies/schengen-borders-and-visa/schengen-area/temporary-reintroduction-border-control_en.
118. The relevant authority is the Hellenic Coastguard, which from an administratively point of view comes under the Ministry of Shipping and Insular Policy. Note that the Hellenic Coastguard may carry and use weapons and firearms.
119. *See* Frontex, Annual Activity Report 2015, Brussels, 28 Jun. 2016, 10659/16, p. 21, at: https://www.statewatch.org/media/documents/news/2016/jul/eu-frontex-2015-activity-report.pdf.
120. *See* Regulation (EC) No. 810/2009 of the European Parliament and of the Council of 13 Jul. 2009 establishing a Community Code on Visas (Visa Code), O.J. L 243, 15.9.2009, p. 1, as each time in force.

# Chapter 2. Right to Enter the Country

## §1. Conditions for the Right to Enter

*58.* Law 5038/2023 does not lay down expressly which are the conditions for foreigners to exercise the right to enter the Greek territory, apart from the requirement to have been issued with an entry visa. In particular, Article 7(1) thereof provides that a third-country national, who enters the Greek territory, must hold a valid travel document which is recognized by the competent Greek authorities and meets the criteria of the aforementioned Schengen Borders Code.[121] The latter has the legal status of an EU regulation and has become part of the domestic legal system of all Member States from 12 April 2016.[122] Article 7(2) adds that the valid travel document must also have an entry visa if so required by the applicable international conventions, EU law or Greek law. Generally speaking, entry visas are distinguished as follows: uniform visas (Visa C); visas with Limited Territorial Validity (Visa VTL); ATV; and long-duration visas (national visa – Visa D).

*59.* Even though not stipulated in Law 5038/2023, the Greek State must observe the pertinent rules of international human rights law when third-country nationals enter its territory. This follows from Article 4 of the aforementioned Regulation 2016/399 (the EU legal instrument on the Schengen Borders Code). It provides that decisions on the entry of third-country nationals must be reached on an individual basis and that Member States must act in full compliance with the relevant EU law (including the Charter of Fundamental Rights of the European Union), with the relevant rules of public international law (including the Convention Relating to the Status of Refugees), with obligations relating to aliens having access to international protection (e.g., the principle of non-refoulement), as well as with fundamental rights. The text of Regulation 2016/399 does not explain what it means by fundamental rights.[123] However, a grammatical interpretation in conjunction with the purpose of Regulation 2016/399 could lead to the conclusion that it means the human rights and the fundamental freedoms that each Member State must observe and give effect to on account of the existence of other treaties to which it is a contracting party (*see also* discussion *supra*).

## §2. Procedures

*60.* The relevant procedures should be distinguished according to whether the alien, who wants to enter into the Greek territory, requires an entry visa or not. As regards the former category, according to Article 7(1) of Law 5038/2023, the examination of requests for the issuance of entry visas is undertaken by the Greek consular authority in whose jurisdiction the third-country national, who has applied for

121. *See* Art. 6 of the aforementioned EU Regulation 2016/399 on entry conditions for third-country nationals.
122. *Ibid.*, Art. 45.
123. *See also ibid.*, preambular para. 36 (‘This Regulation respects fundamental rights … ’).

the visa, legally resides.[124] Effectively this means that, if for the sake of argument, the applicant is legally residing in State X (whether he is also a national of this state or not is not of relevance) but State X comes under the territorial jurisdiction of the Greek consular office that is located in State Y, the application will be examined by the consular office in State Y. It should be mentioned that during the 2010s, when, as explained above, the country had been facing a sovereign debt crisis, which led to an extremely dire economic and financial situation, several Greek embassies and consular offices were closed down as a measure to cut down public expenditure.[125] In the example given above, to obtain an entry visa, the alien will have to leave the state where he resides and go to State Y, which means that State Y must allow him to enter its territory for the purpose of visiting a Greek consular office. Of course, State Y has no obligation to do so.

*61.* The Greek consular office is the competent authority to examine the visa request.[126] Its decision will have to take into account any existing reasons why it should not be granted. This would be the case if granting an entry visa will violate or be against public order, public security and/or public health. Pursuant to Article 7(7) of Law 5038/2023, national entry visas are issued with a period of validity that ranges between ninety-one days and one year, if: (a) the requirements of the aforementioned EU Regulation 810/2009 are met; and (b) all the necessary documents envisaged in the ministerial decision to be issued pursuant to the authority of Article 176(1) have been duly submitted. Regarding the ministerial decision, it should be explained that often Greek laws do not regulate specific areas of law or specific matters in depth, but they only lay down the basic rules or guidelines and authorize the subsequent issuance of ministerial decisions for detailed regulation.[127] The Immigration Code is a typical example of such legislation: Article 176 authorizes the issuance of some sixty-nine different ministerial decisions. In the past, there have been instances where ministerial decisions were adopted with great delay and certainly not within the time frame envisaged in the legislation in question. No doubt, this state of affairs is problematic and has resulted in the Greek State and public

124. Article 7(1) also stipulates that a Greek consular authority shall examine an application which was lodged by a third-country national, who was lawfully present in the third country but who is not residing within the territorial competence of the consular authority, provided that the applicant has sufficiently justified the submission of the application in the consular authority in question.

125. Few of them have since reopened. According to the Ministry of Foreign Affairs, at the time of writing, there eighty-seven Greek diplomatic missions abroad, *see* https://www.mfa.gr/missionsabroad/en/.

126. Note that the collection of the applications for entry visas can be delegated to private companies, *see, e.g.*, the following: 'The Consular Office of the Greek Embassy in Ankara has outsourced the collection of all Schengen visa applications and biometric data to Kosmos Vize. The additional cost of the service fee of 30 Euros is paid directly to Kosmos Vize,' online available at: https://www.mfa.gr/turkey/visas.html?mission=ank&lang=extra1.

127. These are secondary/subsidiary legislative instruments of an executory character (in some jurisdictions they would be referred to as 'by-laws'), whose adoption is entrusted either to a single minister or to more than one ministers. The Hellenic Parliament is not involved in the conclusion and issuance of ministerial decisions, whose legal basis must always be a law that has been promulgated and published in the Official Gazette.

authorities being unable to apply the legislative provisions as they should be. In turn, this has often left in limbo the legal position and status of thousands of immigrants.

*62.* That this state of affairs has been allowed to continue for almost four decades does raise several questions, not least whether the rule of law is truly and genuinely observed in Greece. While any further discussion on this matter goes beyond the scope of the present monograph, suffice to mention that the *Rule of Law Report on Greece*, which the European Commission published in July 2023 was rather critical[128] and, even more so, a Resolution that the European Parliament adopted in February 2024.[129]

*63.* In execution of the aforementioned Article 176(1) of Law 5038/2023, in March 2024 the Minister of Foreign Affairs and the Minister of Immigration and Asylum (but not the Minister of Citizen Protection) adopted Ministerial Decision No. 95391/2024, which sets out the required documentation for issuing not only entry visas but also residence permits.[130] It follows that the relevant provisions of Law 5038/2023 should be read in conjunction with the terms of Ministerial Decision No. 95391/2024. The structure of the latter is as follows: it starts by setting out the general provisions that are applicable to the process of submitting applications for the issuance and renewal of residence permits as well as by laying down the supporting documents that are necessary for the initial grant and renewal of residence permits (Articles 1 and 2 thereof). Thereafter, it sets out the conditions and the requirements for not only issuing entry visas but also specific types of residence permits.

128. *See* European Commission, Commission Staff Working Document, *2023 Rule of Law Report – Country Chapter on the rule of law situation in Greece,* Brussels, 5 Jul. 2023, SWD(2023) 808 final, at: https://commission.europa.eu/publications/2023-rule-law-report-communication-and-country-chapters_en. The 2024 Report was also very critical: 2024 Rule of Law Report: Country Chapter on the rule of law situation in Greece, Brussels, 24 Jul. 2024, SWD(2024) 808 final, at: https://commission.europa.eu/publications/2024-rule-law-report-communication-and-country-chapters_en.

129. European Parliament, Resolution of 7 Feb. 2024 on the rule of law and media freedom in Greece, 2024/2502(RSP) – P9_TA(2024)0069, para. 27, at:https://www.europarl.europa.eu/doceo/document/TA-9-2024-0069_EN.html Among others, it called upon the European Commission 'to make full use of the tools available to it to address the breaches of the values enshrined in Article 2 TEU in Greece'; this provision stipulates that the EU is an international organization which is founded on the values of respect for human dignity, freedom, democracy, equality, the rule of law as well as respect for human rights. *See* further, European Parliament, 'The Protection of Article 2 TEU Values in the EU', Fact Sheets on the European Union – 2024, at: https://www.europarl.europa.eu/ftu/pdf/en/FTU_4.1.2.pdf. Even though European Parliament Resolutions are not legally binding documents, Member States cannot ignore them or pretend that they are not aware of them.

130. *See* Joint Ministerial Decision No. 95391/2024, Determination of the supporting documents, per category of national entry visa, and of the required documentation for the issuance and renewal of residence permits, in accordance with the provisions of Law 5038/2023, FEK 2024, Issue B' No. 1807, as amended by Decision 272153/2024, FEK 2024, Issue B' No. 6201.

*64.* For example, Article 3 of Ministerial Decision No. 95391/2024 concerns the issuance of national entry visas (Visa D) as well as residence permits for third-country nationals, who are employed in the Greek territory with a contract for dependent work or for seasonal work. These residence permits are called Category 'E' and are distinguished into six different and separate types of residence permits, as follows:

a. *Residence Permit Type* E*1*, which is laid down in Article 4 of Ministerial Decision No. 95391/2024. It concerns residence permits that are issued to third-country nationals who will be employed in Greece as highly qualified employees, pursuant to the provisions of EU Directive 2021/1883, the so-called EU Blue Card Directive.[131] It should be noted that Article 4 of Law 5038/2023 defines 'high qualified employment' as follows: the employment of a person, who is protected by Greek labour law as an employee and provides genuine and effective work on behalf of or under the direction of another person, regardless of the legal type of the employment relationship, who is paid for said work and who has the required professional qualifications.
b. *Residence Permit Type E2*: Article 5 of Ministerial Decision No. 95391/2024. It concerns residence permits for third-country nationals in intra-corporate transfers, i.e., foreign employees who move from one company to another. The relevant regulatory framework is pursuant to the provisions of EU Directive 2014/66, which has been mentioned above.[132]
c. *Residence Permit Type E3*: Article 6 of Ministerial Decision No. 95391/2024. It concerns residence permits for special-purpose employment in accordance with Article 59 and Article 60 of Law 5038/2023. In particular, Article 59 pertains to the residence permits that are issued to third-country nationals who fall into the ambit of nine categories of employees. Suffice to mention the following three categories:

   (i) persons who are employed in Greece as managers or as executives[133] of companies, which fall into the scope of Law 2289/1995 and are involved in marine research or in drilling and mining hydrocarbons;[134] (ii) employees and legal representatives who are solely employed by companies that are regulated pursuant to the provisions of Compulsory Law 89/1967 and Compulsory Law 378/1968 on the establishment in Greece of foreign commercial and industrial

131. Directive (EU) 2021/1883 of the European Parliament and of the Council of 20 Oct. 2021 on the conditions of entry and residence of third-country nationals for the purpose of highly qualified employment, and repealing Council Directive 2009/50/EC, O.J. L 382, 28.10.2021, p. 1.
132. Directive 2014/66 on the conditions of entry and residence of third-country nationals in the framework of an intra-corporate transfer, transposed into Greek law under the aforementioned Law 4540/2018.
133. The term 'executives' has been defined in Art. 4 of Law 5038/2023 as a person who holds a senior position and who primarily leads the management of the host entity, under the general supervision or direction of the board of directors or the board of shareholders of the enterprise. Executives are responsible for the supervision and controlling the work of other employees and have the authority to recommend the hiring, firing or other actions relating to the enterprise's personnel.
134. Law 2289/1995, Search, exploration and exploitation of hydrocarbons and other provisions, FEK 1995, Issue A' No. 27, as amended by Law 4819/2021, FEK 2021 Issue A' No. 129.

companies,[135] by Article 25 of Law 27/1975 on the establishment in Greece of offices or branches of foreign shipping companies, as well as by undertakings regulated under Legislative Decree 2687/1953 on investments and the protection of funds abroad; and (iii) managers of investment vehicles that the Greek State considers to be strategic investments according to Article 2(2) of Law 4864/2021.[136] As regards Article 60 of Law 5038/2023, it contains common provisions for issuing and renewing Type E3 residence permits.

d. *Residence Permit Type E4*: Article 7 of Ministerial Decision No. 95391/2024. It concerns residence permits for third-country nationals who are going to reside and work in Greece and who do not fall into the other categories according to Article 61 of Law 5038/2023.
e. *Residence Permit Type E5*: Article 8 of Ministerial Decision No. 95391/2024. It concerns (single) titles for residence and for employment (National Entry Visa – Visa D) for the purpose of seasonal work according to the aforementioned EU Directive 2014/36.
f. *Residence Permit Type E6*: Article 9 of Ministerial Decision No. 95391/2024. It concerns residence permits that are issued to seasonal migrant workers pursuant to Article 66 of Law 5038/2023. More specifically, these are residence permits granted to those third-country nationals, who have entered the Greek territory with a national seasonal work visa and will be employed for a maximum period of nine months within a total period of twelve months.

*65.* Article 7(6) of Law 5038/2023 provides that, in accordance with Article 35 of the aforementioned EU Regulation 810/2009, in exceptional cases, an entry visa may be granted by the competent authorities of the Ministry of Citizen Protection at (external) border points of entry/crossing points upon the arrival of a third-country national. It should be mentioned that Article 7(6) of Law 5038/2023 does not stipulate which are the requirements and the conditions laid down in Article 35 of Regulation 810/2009 because the latter, being an EU Regulation, has been incorporated as such into Greek law without the need for further enactment. Briefly, these conditions and requirements are the following:

a. the third-country national – applicant has been unable to apply for a visa in advance;
b. he is in the position to produce and/or submit documents which substantiate his claim that there exist unforeseeable events and imperative reasons for entering the Greek territory without having secured an entry visa in advance; and
c. his return to the country of origin or the country of last residence has been assessed by the competent authorities to be certain.

---

135. These two legislative instruments have been codified in Law 4864/2021, Strategic investments and improvement of the investment environment through the acceleration of processes in private and strategic investments, creating a framework for technology companies and other urgent provisions for development, FEK 2021 Issue A' No. 237.
136. *Ibid.*

*66.* Neither Regulation 810/2009 nor Law 5038/2023 define what the term 'exceptional cases' means and how should it be understood. Thus, it will be up to the authorities at the border points to rule whether they exist or not, but in each case, adequate justification must be given, especially if the application for entry is dismissed. According to Article 35(3) of EU Regulation 810/2009, visas that are issued at the external borders of Member States entitle the holder to stay for a maximum period of fifteen days, depending on the purpose and conditions of the intended stay. One could think that an 'exceptional case' would be the sudden death of a third-country national and the need for his close relatives to come to Greece to arrange for the funeral or for the repatriation of the body, etc.

*67.* It is a rule of general application that all decisions, which are issued by Greek diplomatic and consular authorities and reject applications for the issuance of entry visas, must be justified and reasoned. However, Article 7(4) of Law 5038/2023 provides that, subject to reasons of public order and public security, specific and detailed reasoning must always be given when the decisions rejecting applications have been filed by the following categories of third-country nationals:

a. third-country nationals who are family members of a Greek national. Which individuals will be considered 'family members' is laid down in Article 4 of Law 5038/2023. Suffice to mention that they include the spouse of a Greek national; the person with whom a Greek citizen has entered into a cohabitation agreement that was drawn up in Greece or abroad before a Greek consular authority; and, regardless of nationality, the descendants who are relatives by blood in a direct line to spouses or partners having Green nationality and who are under 21 years of age or, regardless of age, as long as they are still dependent on said spouses or partners;
b. third-country nationals, who are family members of a person having the citizenship of another EU Member State (restrictions apply here);
c. third-country nationals, whose entry, residence, settlement and employment in Greece has been requested pursuant to the provisions of EU law; and
d. third-countries nationals, who are employed in companies established in another EU Member State and who move to Greece for the purpose of carrying out contractual obligations relating to their employment. In cases (c) and (d), it is rather obvious that the EU wants to promote the interests of EU-based companies regardless of whether they employ EU nationals or third-country nationals.

*68.* As regards the second category, namely third-country nationals, who are not required to have an entry visa, Article 7(5) of Law 5038/2023 provides that, subject to the provisions of the European Travel Information and Authorization System (ETIAS), they are allowed to enter and to remain in the Greek territory for a period of time not exceeding ninety days within any one period of 180 days. It follows that if they remain for ninety-one or more days, a residence permit is mandatory and if the third-country national is not in possession of one, technically he is an illegal/irregular foreigner. At the time of writing, ETIAS was not yet in operation, but it should become operative during the first half of 2025. The idea behind ETIAS is that the people coming to EU Member States from the over sixty visa-exempt countries[137] (their total population is estimated at 1.4 billion people) should have obtained travel authorization for entry before they travel to an EU Member State. This is of course not a novel process and has been imposed for many years now by the USA and other states as a compulsory requirement for traveling and entering their territories.

*69.* Third-country nationals entering Greece for tourism or to attend conferences, cultural and sporting events, etc., and generally for short-duration stays, are allowed to temporarily enter and remain in the Greek territory without having to be issued with a residence permit. The only condition is that the consular visa that they hold is still valid. In the case of third-country nationals, who have been permitted to enter the Greek territory without a visa, they are allowed to stay for a period of up to ninety days within any period of 180 days. Pursuant to Article 7(5) of Law 5038/2023, the period of validity of a visa that has been issued or the permitted length of the stay can be extended in accordance with Article 33 of Regulation 810/2009, if the visa holder fulfils two basic criteria. The first is that he has adequate means of living and also provides evidence of a force majeure situation or that there are humanitarian reasons that prevented him from leaving the Schengen area before the end of the visa's validity period or the permitted length of stay, as the case might be. The second is that he invokes reasons relating to the fulfilment of international obligations that are based on inter-state agreements.

*70.* The extension shall be granted by means of a decision to be adopted by the Ministry of Citizen Protection. It should be noted that even though the visa was originally issued by a consular office, the Ministry of Foreign Affairs is not involved in these cases. Reference should also be made to Article 33(4) of Regulation 810/2009; it provides that the authority that shall be competent to extend the visa shall be that of the EU Member State on whose territory the third-country national is present at the moment of applying for the extension. It follows that Greece may be asked to extend entry visas that have been issued by another EU Member State, while third EU Member States may be petitioned to lengthen visas that were originally issued by Greek consular authorities. It follows that the competent authorities on migration in the 27 EU countries must not only cooperate among them but must also trust each other.

137. *See* Regulation (EU) 2018/1806 of the European Parliament and of the Council of 14 Nov. 2018 listing the third countries whose nationals must be in possession of visas when crossing the external borders and those whose nationals are exempt from that requirement O.J. L 303 28.11.2018, p. 39, as lastly amended by Regulation (EU) 2023/850 of the European Parliament and of the Council of 19 Apr. 2023, O.J. L 110, 25.4.2023, p. 1.

## Chapter 3. Refusal of Entry

*71.* The basic rule concerning refusal of the entry of third-country nationals into the Greek territory is laid down in Article 6(1) of Law 5038/2023. It reads as follows: 'The Greek control authorities can prohibit, by giving reasons, the entry into Greece of a third country citizen, if he does not meet the conditions of entry, as these are defined in Regulation (EU) 2016/399 'Schengen Borders Code', as it is each time in force.'[138] Even though the Immigration Code is a legislative instrument that is principally aimed at regulating what third-country nationals are allowed to do or are not allowed to do before and after they have entered the Greek territory, it is interesting to note that the fifth paragraph of Article 6 provides that entry into the Greek territory shall not be prohibited to anyone who proves to have Greek citizenship or is a national of another EU Member State, even if he is not in possession of a passport or other travel document. Arguably, this is a stipulation that ought to have been envisaged in the Greek Constitution.

*72.* In case the conditions for entry as per Article 6(1) of Law 5038/2023are not met, the second paragraph of Article 6 provides that the third country citizen shall be served with a reasoned decision, which will be in the standardized form to be found in Part B of Annex V of Regulation 2016/399. The reasons on the basis of which entry was refused must be mentioned in the decision. However, under Article 6(3) therefore, despite the existence of reasons that would have ordinarily prohibited entrance, the Minister of Citizen Protection is empowered to allow the entrance of third-country citizens, who are at external border crossing points, in the following three situations: (a) if it is required for serious reasons of public interest; (b) if it is necessary for reasons of force majeure; or (c) if it is required for the movement of vessel (ships) and it cannot be done in any other way.[139] The fourth paragraph of Article 6 regulates the entry of a rather specific category of third-country nationals, namely those who have entered Greece from a transit zone and have not been

138. Regarding the reference 'as it is each time in force', note that, at the time Law 5038/2023 had been promulgated, Regulation 2016/399 had not been amended and, at the time of writing, it was still not amended. However, on 14 Dec. 2021, the European Commission presented a Proposal for a Regulation of the European Parliament and of the Council amending Regulation (EU) 2016/399 on a Union Code on the rules governing the movement of persons across borders, COM(2021) 891 final. This proposal was originally announced in the European Commission s Pact on Migration and Asylum; *see* Communication from the Commission on a New Pact on Migration and Asylum, COM/2020/609 final, 23 Sep. 2020. On 20 Dec. 2023, a political agreement was reached on the Pact by the European Parliament and the Council of the EU. On 6 Feb. 2024, the Council of the EU and the European Parliament reached a provisional agreement to amend the Schengen Borders Code. Finally, on 24 May 2024 the Council gave its final approval to a new Schengen Borders Code: Regulation (EU) 2024/1717 of the European Parliament and of the Council of 13 Jun. 2024 amending Regulation (EU) 2016/399 on a Union Code on the rules governing the movement of persons across borders, O.J. L, 2024/1717, 20.6.2024.

139. Note that Law 5038/2023 uses the term 'force majeure' in six different provisions but does not contain a definition of this term. Therefore, what constitutes and what does not constitute 'force majeure' should be examined on a case to cases basis by the competent State authorities and their determination should be open to judicial review before the relevant administrative court of justice. As regards the movement of vessels as an exception reason, this is explained by the fact that Greek interests possess the second largest merchant fleet in the world.

allowed entry into the country of destination. In case these individuals had been in a third country before entering the Greek territory, they shall not be accepted for re-entry if they do not fulfil anew the aforementioned conditions.

*73.* Finally, Article 6(6) of Law 5038/2023 deals with those instances where a third country citizen, who is already a holder of a residence permit, has left Greece and upon his arrival to enter the Greek territory again, the competent authorities establish the presence of reasons which justify the withdrawal of the residence permit or that his request to have the residency permit renewed has been rejected. In these instances, the entry of the third-country national will not be allowed until a final decision on the revocation or rejection of the residence permit has been issued.

# Part II. Residence Rights: General Provisions

## Chapter 1. Short Stay

*74.* Third-country nationals do not require obtaining a residence permit if their stay is for a short period of time, which is defined as a period not exceeding ninety days in any period of 180 days. This applies, for example, to tourists, to participants in conferences symposia, etc., and to spectators of sporting events. This does not mean, however, that they will not need an entry visa. Indeed, as has been explained above, Greece is part of the Schengen area, and its external borders are at the same time the external borders of the EU. Therefore, Greece may not determine unilaterally whom and under which conditions to allow to enter its territory but has to follow the relevant EU rules and procedures, including for short stay. If Greece wanted to deviate from these EU rules, it had to seek permission from the European Commission. It follows that, even for short stays, Greece will have to ask for dispensation, which may or may not be granted and which should not be permanent but allowed for a specific period of time.

*75.* In 2012, the European Commission approved a special visa agreement, which had been concluded between Greece and Turkey, allowing Turkish nationals to visit certain Greek islands located in the Aegean Sea for brief periods of time by not requiring to have already secured an entry visa from one of the Greek Consulates in Turkey but by having their passports stamped by the Greek Police once they were on these Greek islands. In effect, this was a fast-track temporary visa, which originally ran for a trial period of four years. After the European Commission discontinued it in 2016, Greece lobbied to have the scheme reinstated. It claimed that these Aegean Sea islands relied on tourism and given that had been particularly hit by the refugee crisis from Turkey in the period 2015–2016 (*see supra)*, this express visa regime would create considerable wealth for the local economies. In April 2018, the European Commission approved the continuation of the scheme, which was broadened to also include third-country nationals who were living legally in Turkey.

*76.* On 7 December 2023, the fifth meeting of the Supreme (High-Level) Cooperation Council between the Republic of Turkey and the Hellenic Republic took place. At the end of it, the Athens Declaration on Friendly Relations and Good-Neighbourliness was signed by the two states.[140] They agreed to engage in continuous constructive and meaningful consultations covering several areas or 'pillars'. The one that is of relevance here is the so-called Positive Agenda, which is part of a strengthened Joint Action Plan, which includes measures of common interest in the fields of, *inter alia*, tourism. It should be noted that the text of the Declaration expressly states that it is not an international agreement, that it does not bind either parties under international law and that nothing in it may be construed as creating any legal rights or obligations for the two sides.

*77.* Notwithstanding the political character of this Declaration, during the meeting of the Cooperation Council, some fifteen agreements and memoranda of agreement were signed and '[a] public announcement was made regarding the prospect of reactivation and expansion of a former pilot scheme for the granting of seven-day visas to Turkish citizens at the point of entry in ten (10) Greek islands of the Eastern Aegean Sea'.[141] Following consultations between the Greek government and the European Commission, in April 2024 this express visa programme was extended to ten Aegean Sea islands. Presently, the programme is due to expire at the end of March 2025. Each entry visa costs EUR 60, it can be issued at any time in the Greek island port of arrival and takes the form of a special stamp placed on the passport. Visitors from Turkey who enter the Greek territory with such a visa are not allowed to leave the country and travel to any other destination inside the EU. Until now, this programme has been the only exception to the entry visa system that applies to the whole of the Schengen area.

---

140. Text at: https://www.primeminister.gr/en/2023/12/07/33195.
141. *See* Ministry of Foreign Affairs of the Hellenic Republic, 'Türkiye', online available at: https://www.mfa.gr/en/bilateral-relations/turkiye/.

## Chapter 2. Long Stay

### §1. Conditions

*78.* The long stay of third-country nationals who legally reside in the Greek territory, including holders of international protection, is regulated in Articles 143 et seq. of Law 5038/2023.[142] This is a matter for which the EU has adopted rules and procedures that apply to all Member States. Therefore, Articles 143 et seq. are in effect the provisions that have implemented in the Greek legal order the relevant instruments of EU law, namely Council Directive 2003/109,[143] as it has been amended by the aforementioned Directive 2011/51, by virtue of which it covers the beneficiaries of international protection as well.[144] According to Article 143(2), these provisions of the Immigration Code do not apply, *inter alia*, to third-country nationals who have been issued a residence permit for studies or work training or who have received a residence permit in Greece under the rules of temporary protection or who enjoy the legal status of the Vienna Convention on Diplomatic Relations (1961),[145] or the aforementioned Vienna Convention on Consular Relations (1963). However, pursuant to Article 143(3), these provisions do apply, subject to more favourable provisions, to those third-country nationals who come under the ambit of the following treaties: (a) bilateral and multilateral agreements that have been concluded between the EU Member States or between the EU and its Member States on the one hand and third countries on the other hand; (b) bilateral and multilateral agreements concluded between Greece and third countries; (c) two treaties adopted under the auspices of the Council of Europe, namely the aforementioned European Convention on Establishment and the European Social Charter; and (d) paragraph 11 of the Annex to the (United Nations) Convention relating to the Status of Refugees,[146] as amended by the Protocol of New York Protocol relating to the Status of Refugees.[147]

*79.* The conditions for third-country nationals to obtain the status of long-term resident and to be issued with the so-called residence permit type M1 are laid down in Article 144 of Law 5038/2023. This type of permit is only available to third-country nationals, who have resided in Greece lawfully and continuously for five

142. For a specimen of a Greek national visa for long stay, *see* https://www.mfa.gr/images/docs/ethnikes_theoriseis/application_national_visas.pdf.
143. Council Directive 2003/109/EC of the Council of 25 Nov. 2003 concerning the status of third-country nationals who are long-term residents, OJ L 16, 23.1.2004, p. 44.
144. Directive 2011/51 amending Council Directive 2003/109/EC to extend its scope to beneficiaries of international protection, OJ L 132, 19.5.2011, p. 1.
145. Done on 18 Apr. 1961, entered into force on 24 Apr. 1964, 500 *U.N.T.S.* 95. Greece ratified it under Legislative Decree 503/1970, FEK 1970 Issue A' No. 108.
146. Signed on 28 Jul. 1951, entered into force on 22 Apr. 1954, 189 *U.N.T.S.* 137. Greece ratified it under Legislative Decree 3989/1959, FEK 1959 Issue A' No. 201.
147. Signed on 31 Jan. 1967, entered into force 4 Oct. 1967, 606 *U.N.T.S.* 267. Greece ratified it under Compulsory Law 389/1968, FEK 1968 Issue A' No. 125.

years immediately before the submission of the relevant application.[148] Moreover, all the following conditions must be met:

a. the applicant has sufficient income for his own needs and for those of his family; this income should not derive from emoluments received from Greece's social assistance system. By 'sufficient income' the Immigration Code means an amount that cannot be less than the annual salary of a salaried person who is paid the minimum wage,[149] increased by 10% for all dependent members of his family, but including any regular unemployment benefit that he may receive. Moreover, any contributions by family members are taken into account in the calculation of the applicant's income, which is from the fulfilment of his social security and tax obligations;
b. the applicant and all family members have full health insurance that covers the same risks for which Greek nationals are covered; and
c. the applicant meets the conditions for integration into Greek society, in accordance with the second paragraph of Article 145 of Law 5038/2023. This provision stipulates that a third-country national is deemed to be integrated if any of the following three conditions apply: (a) he proves that he has sufficient knowledge of the Greek language as well as knowledge of elements of Greek history and culture (as further stipulated in Article 160 of Law 5038/2023);[150] or (b) he holds a permanent residence card as a member of a Greek family; or (c) he has lived lawfully in Greece for a period of twelve years.

### §2. Procedures

*80.* One of the main problems that third-country nationals, especially migrant workers, experience in Greece is access to reliable and updated information and the language barrier. Unlike other European states, Greek legislation almost in its entirety is not translated into foreign languages, while public authorities use the Greek language most of the time, which is very difficult to comprehend and learn. Pursuant to Article 144(4) of Law 5038/2023, it will be the Ministry of Immigration and Asylum as well as the competent public authorities examining and granting residence permit applications that will inform interested immigrants about the

148. Periods of absence of less than six consecutive months that do not exceed in total ten months within the five-year period are included for the calculation of the five-year period.
149. Since 1 Apr. 2024, the gross minimum monthly salary for those employed in the private sector in Greece has been set by the government at EUR 830; the annual minimum salary can be found by multiplying the monthly salary by fourteen. If the employee is married, his salary is increased by 10% and for every three years in employment he is entitled to an additional 10% on the gross salary.
150. Article 160 of Law 5038/2023 provides that the adequate knowledge of the Greek language, history and culture can be demonstrated if the applicant is in possession of one of the academic titles mentioned therein, including a title that shows that he completed compulsory schooling in Greece (nine years); a graduation certificate from a high school abroad, which is a part of the Greek education system; a degree from the Greek language department of a foreign university; or a Greek State language certificate (at least level B1 according to the Common European Framework of Reference for Languages).

conditions and procedures for obtaining the long-term resident status, for the rights and obligations that derive from it, etc.[151]

*81*. Under Article 145(1) and (3) of Law 5038/2023, the application for acquiring the status of long-term resident must be lodged with the public authority that granted the last residence permit. This entity, after requesting the opinion of the relevant police authority for matters relating to public order and public security, examines whether the aforementioned Article 144 conditions are met and should issue the residence permit type M1 at the latest within six months from the day the fully documented application was submitted; an extension of three months may be given, if there are reasons that justify it. Should there be a positive decision, the third-country national will be issued the residence permit, in accordance with EU Regulation 1030/2002.[152]

*82*. Pursuant to Article 147 of Law 5038/2023, the examination of reasons concerning public order and public safety is a prerequisite for issuing a decision on the long-term resident application and, subsequently, granting the residence permit. In particular, when making the relevant decision, the seriousness or the nature of the offence against public order or public security committed by the applicant or the risk associated with him will be taken into consideration but so will the length of his stay in Greece as well the existence of any ties with the country. The interpretation to be given to this provision is that the commission of crimes by the third-country national is a negative consideration for his application but it should not be rejected on this ground alone, if there are other facts showing strong links with Greece, for example, he has resided in Greece for many years, he got married and his children were born and raised in Greece, he has a steady employment, etc. Finally, Article 174 provides that the refusal to grant a long-term residence permit may not be based on reasons associated with Greece's fiscal policy.

*83*. The right of appeal against decisions rejecting applications for long-term residence permits or for decisions revoking the same is regulated in Article 151 of Law 5038/2023. The first paragraph provides that all such decisions must be reasoned, they must be notified to the interested parties and must be accompanied by information on the legal remedy that is available as well as the deadline for exercising it. The legal remedy in question is the one envisaged in Article 24 of Law 2690/1999, which contains the Code of Administrative Procedures.[153] Pursuant to

151. Note, access to legal aid and legal representation is foreseen, as is explained below.
152. Council Regulation (EC) No. 1030/2002 of 13 Jun. 2002 laying down a uniform format for residence permits for third-country nationals, OJ L 157, 15.6.2002, p. 1, as last amended by Council Regulation (EU) 2017/1954 of the European Parliament and of the Council of 25 Oct. 2017, O.J. L 286, 1.11.2017, p. 9.
153. The purpose of the Code of Administrative Procedures, which was lastly amended under Law 4962/2022, FEK 2022 Issue A' No, 148, is to lay down provisions that regulate the administrative actions and other transactions that take place between the population, on the one hand, and the Greek State, local self-government (municipalities, prefectures, etc.) as well as other legal entities that are governed under public law, on the other hand. The provisions of the Code apply equally to Greek nationals and aliens, the latter having the same protection and the same remedies as the former.

the relevant administrative procedures regarding long-term residence permits, the affected third-country national is entitled to request from the public authority that issued the administrative act (in our case the decision rejecting the application for a long-term residence permit) to annul it or amend it. The public authority in question must deliver its decision within thirty days and notify the third-country national concerned. Often public authorities do not reply within the thirty-day period, and, legally speaking, this is construed as having rejected the application. According to Article 151(3) of Law 5038/2023, the decisions rejecting applications for granting long-term residence permits or for revoking the same are open to judicial review (effectively an action for annulment) before the competent administrative court of justice. The applicable provisions are laid down in Article 15 of Law 3068/2002,[154] as was lastly revised by Article 57(1) of Law 4689/2020.[155]

*84.* More specifically, actions for annulment against decisions, which were issued by public authorities (these will be the 'individual administrative acts' mentioned *supra*) pursuant to the domestic legislation on aliens, fall into the jurisdiction of the three-member administrative Court of First Instance in whose territorial competence the public authority that issued the challenged act is seated. The judgments delivered by three-member administrative courts of first instance are subject to appeal before the Council of State.[156] Finally, it is allowed for third-country nationals to request the suspension of the administrative act's execution before the action for annulment has been lodged. The relevant provision is Article 15(6) of Law 3068/2002: such requests may only exceptionally be filed before the competent three-member administrative Court of First Instance and, if filed, the action for annulment must be lodged within the next thirty days.

## §3. Duration and Loss

*85.* In accordance with Article 148(1) of Law 5038/2023, the status of long-term resident shall be revoked or lost, among others, in the following circumstances: (a) if it is proven that the third-country national has acted fraudulently and conspired to obtain this status; (b) if he has been away from the territory of the EU for a period of twelve consecutive months or longer; (c) if he constitutes a threat to Greek public order, taking into account the seriousness of the offences he has committed; (d) by having exercised the right of residence in another Member State, he

154. Law 3068/2002, Compliance of the Greek public administration with the decisions of the courts of justice, FEK 2002 Issue A' No. 274.
155. Law 4689/2020, Incorporation into Greek legislation of Directives (EU) 2016/800, 2017/1371, 2017/541, 2016/1919, 2014/57/EU, ratification of the Memorandum of Administrative Cooperation between the Ministry of Justice of the Hellenic Republic and the Ministry of Justice and Public Order of the Republic of Cyprus, amendments to Law 3663/2008 so as to implement Regulation (EU) 2018/1727 and other provisions, FEK 2020 Issue A' No. 103.
156. *See* Art. 15(5) of Law 3068/2002, as amended, in conjunction with Art. 5 of Law 702/1977 on Administrative Courts of Justice and the Council of State, as presently in force.

has acquired the status of a long-term resident in another EU Member State pursuant to the terms of the aforementioned Directive 2003/109;[157] or (e) if it proven that he had been absent from the Greek territory for a period exceeding six years. However, Article 149 of Law 5038/2023 stipulates that the status of long-term resident may be restored in the above cases (b) and (d). To do so, the third-country national in question must submit an application to the public authority that had initially granted him the long-term resident status and accompany it with the supporting documents that are necessary for issuing the decision envisaged in the aforementioned Article 176(1) of Law 5038/2023. The procedure laid down in Articles 145 and 146 of Law 5038/2023 shall apply here as well.

*86.* Reference should be made to the position of British nationals residing in Greece following the withdrawal of the United Kingdom from the EU (the so-called Brexit). Before the United Kingdom withdrew from the EU, a Withdrawal Agreement had been concluded to regulate its future relationship with the EU and the remaining Member States. Immigration was one of the subjects covered.[158] Even though after 31 January 2020, British nationals should have been regarded as third-country nationals, the fact that for so many decades there had been free movement of persons between the UK and the other Member States, that the people who had exercised the freedom of movement had obvious vested interests in their host country, that many marriages had taken place between British nationals and other Member States' nationals, etc., presumably justified that the residence of UK nationals be regulated differently from all other third-country nationals. The provisions in the Withdrawal Agreement subscribe to the principle of reciprocity, in other words, the regulation of immigration applies in exactly the same way to both UK nationals and EU citizens. In particular, Article 15 of the Withdrawal Agreement (it is titled 'Right of permanent residence') provides that those EU citizens and UK nationals (including family members), who have resided legally in the host country (i.e., either in the UK or in one of the twenty-seven EU Member States) in accordance with EU law for a continuous period of five years,[159] shall have the right to reside permanently in the host country under the conditions set out in Articles 16, 17 and 18 of Directive 2004/38, this being the legislative instrument regulating the free movement of people in the EU.[160] Once the right of permanent residence has been acquired it shall be lost only through absence from the host country for more than five consecutive years.

157. Council Directive 2003/109 concerning the status of third-country nationals who are long-term residents, O.J. L 16, 23.1.2004, p. 44, amended by Directive 2011/51 which extended its scope to the beneficiaries of international protection, O.J. L 132, 19.5.2011, p. 1.

158. Agreement on the withdrawal of the United Kingdom of Great Britain and Northern Ireland from the European Union and the European Atomic Energy Community, O.J. C 384I, 12.11.2019, p. 1, entered into force on 31 Jan. 2020.

159. *See* further Art. 16 of the Withdrawal Agreement.

160. Directive 2004/38/EC of the European Parliament and of the Council of 29 Apr. 2004 on the right of citizens of the Union and their family members to move and reside freely within the territory of the Member States amending Regulation No. 1612/68 and repealing Directives 64/221/EEC, 68/360/EEC, 72/194/EEC, 73/148/EEC, 75/34/EEC, 75/35/EEC, 90/364/EEC, 90/365/EEC and 93/96/EEC, O.J. L 158, 30.4.2004, p. 77. The text of Directive 2004/38 was codified by Regulation 492/2011 of the European Parliament and of the Council of 5 Apr. 2011 on freedom of movement

*87.* Furthermore, Article 18 of the Withdrawal Agreement ('Issuance of residence documents') provides that the host country *may* require EU citizens or UK nationals as well as family members to apply for a new residence status in order to be conferred the rights under the Withdrawal Agreement, in which case a document evidencing such status which may be in a digital form, subject to the conditions laid down therein. It follows that this new residence status becomes the basis for legal residence in the host country (emphasis added). However, if a host country does not require EU citizens or UK nationals and family members residing in its territory to apply for the new residence status, they shall have the right to receive, in accordance with Directive 2004/38, a residence document. The EU legislative instrument regarding these documents was adopted in February 2020.[161] It stipulates that the residence documents laid down in Article 18 shall have the uniform format for residence permits for third-country nationals according to the aforementioned Regulation 1030/2002 and annex, as each time in force.[162]

*88.* Based on the above, as of 1 January 2021, the rules for UK nationals and family members living in Greece have distinguished them into two categories: (a) those who are covered by the Withdrawal Agreement, in the sense that they have exercised the right to free movement of people and have lived in the EU prior to 31 December 2020 (they are referred to as 'WA beneficiaries');[163] and (b) those who are not covered by the Withdrawal Agreement and move to Greece for residency, study or work after 31 December 2020. The general rule is that the provisions of the Immigration Code shall be applied to UK nationals and family members (the latter irrespective of whether they are UK nationals or third-country nationals) who have entered the Greek territory after 1 January 2021, subject to any more favourable provisions that have been agreed bilaterally.[164] The validity of the residence

---

for workers within the Union, O.J. L 141, 27.5.2011, p. 1, as last modified by Regulation 2019/1149 of the European Parliament and of the Council of 20 Jun. 2019 establishing a European Labour Authority, amending Regulations (EC) No. 883/2004, (EU) No. 492/2011, and (EU) 2016/589 and repealing Decision (EU) 2016/344, O.J. L 186, 11.7.2019, p. 21.

161. Commission Implementing Decision (EU) 2022/1945 of 21 Feb. 2020 on documents to be issued by Member States pursuant to Art. 18(1) and (4) and Art. 26 of the Agreement on the withdrawal of the United Kingdom of Great Britain and Northern Ireland from the European Union and the European Atomic Energy Community (notified under document C(2020) 1114), C/2020/1114, O.J. L 268, 14.10.2022, p. 26.

162. Council Regulation 1030/2002 laying down a uniform format for residence permits for third-country nationals, as last amended by Regulation 2017/1954.

163. The process to be followed by those UK nationals and family members, who were residing in Greece and wished to remain in the country after Brexit and to acquire the new residence documents envisaged in the Withdrawal Agreement, was laid down in Joint Ministerial Decision of the Minister of Citizen Protection and the Minister of Migration and Asylum 4000/1/113-a' of 19 Oct. 2020, Designation of competent authorities to issue residence documents to the citizens of the United Kingdom and their family members, as well as more specific issues for the implementation of the Agreement on the withdrawal of the United Kingdom from the European Union, FEK 2020 Issue B' No. 4610.

164. *See* Art. 2(8) of Law 4652/2020, Arrangements for the withdrawal of the United Kingdom from the European Union and other provisions, FEK 2020 Issue A' No. 9.

permits to be issued to 'WA beneficiaries', who have acquired the right of permanent residence in Greece, pursuant to Articles 15 and 16 of the Withdrawal Agreement, is ten years and for those who have not acquired the right of permanent residence pursuant to said Articles, is five years.

*89.* Finally, it should be mentioned that the possibility had been given to UK citizens and members of their family, who had been legally resident in Greece for a continuous period of five years, to enjoy the right to permanent residence if they had applied for a five-year residence permit until 31 December 2020. This permit is automatically renewed for five-year intervals. The issuing of this type of residence permit was subject to the non-existence of grounds of public policy and public security that would have led the Greek authorities to reject the application.[165] Finally, it should be noted that some provisions affecting the UK-EU migration and vice versa were included in the bilateral Trade and Cooperation Agreement, which was signed on 30 December 2020 and entered into force on 1 May 2021.[166]

165. *See ibid.*, Art. 2(5).
166. Trade and Cooperation Agreement between the European Union and the European Atomic Energy Community, of the one part, and the United Kingdom of Great Britain and Northern Ireland, of the other part, signed on 30 Dec. 2020, entered in to force on 1 May 2021, O.J. L 149, 30.4.2021, p. 10.

## Chapter 3. Permanent Residence

*90.* There are basically two instances of permanent residence envisaged in the Greek legislation. The first concerns EU Members States' nationals and members of their family and is examined in Part III Chapter 1. The second deals with those third-country nationals, who as investors in immovable property (real estate) and subject to certain conditions, may be issued with a so-called investors permanent residence permit – residency permit Type B.5. This is the so-called golden visa scheme through which foreigners acquired the right to reside in Greece for very long periods of time.

*91.* In Greece, the scheme was introduced in 2013 as a measure to increase foreign investment and augment public revenue at a time when the country was experiencing acute monetary and economic problems and was unable to service its galloping public debt. The scheme has led to serious social problems, especially in the capital city of Athens, where 40% of the population resides and where young people and young couples have been unable to find affordable housing, which is often cited as a main reason for the country's very low fertility rate.[167] In a nutshell, as initially applied, the golden visa programme awarded five-year residency rights to third-country nationals, including spouse and children under the age of 21, who had bought immovable property in Greece whose purchase price was only EUR 250,000. The great advantage of being issued a golden visa in the EU is that holders acquire immediately visa-free access in the whole of the Schengen Zone.

*92.* Effectively, this means that if a third-country national aims at entering, for example, Luxembourg but is unable to do so, he could be issued a 'Gold visa' in Greece and then travel without any restrictions to the desired destination. Moreover, considering that until 2024 the minimum amount of investment for a golden visa in Greece was considerably lower than in other EU Member States, third-country nationals may have opted to invest in Greece, an argument that shows the possible existence of competition between EU Member States. Finally, it should be noted that a 'Gold visa', which has been issued in Greece, offers eligibility for citizenship after only seven years of residency. It is estimated that only in the period from 2021 to 2023 'Gold visas' generated in Greece investments of around EUR 4.3 billion.[168]

*93.* Article 100 of Law 5038/2023 brought some considerable changes to the golden visa scheme. In particular, it doubled the minimum amount of the real estate investment required for the greater Athens region, for Thessaloniki (the second largest city in Greece) and for two islands in the Aegean Sea, raising it to EUR 500,000.

---

167. Note that in 2019 the minimum gross monthly salary in Greece was EUR 650; it was raised to EUR 713 in May 2022 and to EUR 830 in April 2024. Recently, the government announced an increase in 2025, but is still one of the lowest in the EU.

168. Note that the property transfer tax in Greece is 3% of the value of the property as stated in the written transfer contract, which is compulsory drawn up by a notary public. However, it is common knowledge that the purchase price on the contract is considerably less that the actual price of sale.

It also provided that the minimum amount must be spent by acquiring only one immovable property and by acquiring several smaller apartments. However, the social problem of securing adequate and affordable housing for the Greek population, especially those in their 20s and early 30s, has persisted.[169] As has been mentioned *supra*, in April 2024, the Greek Parliament replaced the provisions of Article 100.[170] Under the new rules, which are contained in an unrelated legislative instrument, a Type B.5 residence permit shall be granted to a third-country national for five years, with the possibility of renewal, when the following conditions are met: (a) he has legally entered the country with an entry visa or he happens to reside legally in the Greek territory and irrespective of whether the residence permit he holds does not allow any changes in the purpose of his residency; (b) he fully owns and possesses real estate property in Greece either personally or through a legal entity which is based in Greece or in another EU Member State and whose shares he owns in their entirety; and (c) the minimum value of the property at the time it was acquired was EUR 800,000 for the metropolitan areas of Athens and of Thessaloniki as well as for those islands whose population is more than 3,100 inhabitants; for all other parts of the country the minimum value of the property was set at EUR 400,000.

*94.* In order to maintain the residence permit and to be able to renew it for a five-year term, new obligations were introduced. In particular, the new Article 100(7)(A) of Law 5038/2023 provides that the properties, which have been acquired by third-country nationals for the initial granting or for renewing a real estate investor's residence permit, may not be rented out short-term in the context of the so-called sharing economy (e.g., the so-called Airbnb spaces) and may not be used as the legal seat of a company. Should the third-country national not abide by these obligations/ prohibitions, an administrative fine of EUR 50,000 or EUR 150,000 shall be imposed upon the owner/owners of the property and the residence permit shall be revoked. Furthermore, under Article 100(8)–(9), the resale of the real estate during the validity period of the residence permit to another third-country national is possible. Were this to happen, the right to be granted a type B.5 residence permit will be transferred to the new buyer, and the seller's residence permit shall be simultaneously revoked.

*95.* Given that type B.5 residence permit does not entitle the holder to have access to any form of work, it follows that the third-country national with a revoked

169. Generally, *see* E. Relman, 'The Golden Age of Golden Visas Is over in Southern Europe', *Business Insider*, 9 May 2024, at: https://www.businessinsider.com/golden-visas-greece-portugal-spain-boosted-economy-housing-crisis-2024-5.

170. *See* Art. 64 of Law 5100/2024, Transposition of Directive (EU) 2022/2523 of the Council of 14 Dec. 2022 on ensuring a global minimum level of taxation for multinational enterprise groups and large-scale domestic groups in the European Union (Pillar II) and other urgent provisions, FEK 2024 Issue A' No. 49. The transposed EU legislation was Council Directive 2022/2523 of 14 Dec. 2022 on ensuring a global minimum level of taxation for multinational enterprise groups and large-scale domestic groups in the Union, O.J. L 328, 22.12.2022, p. 1. *See* further, Ministerial Decision 75166/2024, Redesignation of the competent authority for issuing the residence permits provided for in the provisions of Art. 100 of Law 5038/2023 as well as the regulation of more specific matters for the issuance of these residence permits, FEK 2024 Issue B' No. 1596.

permit is no longer considered to be an investor. Unless he is able to apply for and be granted a different type of residence permit, he (and his family members) will have to leave the Greek territory immediately, as his presence will no longer be lawful. However, there might be different applicable scenarios, for example, a member of his family might have been issued a residence permit in his own right and therefore the former investor might be able to remain in Greece as a third-country national who is supported by a close relative with a residence permit; or child of the investor might have been born in Greece and at the age of 17 he acquired Greek citizenship, in which case the child will be the sponsor of his parent. Finally, it should be noted that investor's residence permits, which had been issued to third-country nationals under the legislation in force at the time they were granted,[171] continue to be valid and need not be re-issued. Upon expiration, they shall be extended pursuant to the conditions that were laid down in the legislation in force at the time of issuance, and not under the aforementioned provisions of Law 5038/2023.

171. *See* Art. 20(B) of Law 4251/2014 (the Immigration and Social Integration Code), and Art. 92 of Law 5007/2022, Integrated System for the Provision of Alleviative Care, Arrangements to Respond to the COVID-19 Pandemic and to Protect Public Health, and Other Emergency Arrangements, FEK 2022 Issue A' 241.

# Part III. Residence Rights: Specific Provisions

## Chapter 1. Nationalities with Preferential Treatment: EU Citizens

*96.* Pursuant to Article 162 of Law 5038/2023, so-called titles of residency or residence cards (the term 'residence permit' is not used here) may be issued to EU nationals and members of their family, irrespective of nationality, in accordance with the relevant provisions of Presidential Decree 106/2007, the legal instrument regulating the EU fundamental principle of freedom of movement and residence,[172] which incorporated and implemented domestically the aforementioned Directive 2004/38, also known as the 'Citizens' Rights Directive' or the 'Free Movement Directive'. More specifically, under Article 13 of Presidential Decree 106/2007, citizens of EU Members States and of the EEA (as well as the Swiss Confederation), who have resided legally for a continuous period of five years in Greece, as well as their family members, who have legally resided with them for a continuous period of five years as well, have the right to permanent residence. It should be noted that the nationality of the family members is irrelevant.

*97.* The requirement of continuous residence is rather favourably regulated. For example, it will not be affected even if the person concerned has been out of the Greek territory for a total of six months per year (these are considered to be 'temporary absences'). But even in the case of longer absences, these can be justified, if they were spent, for example, in order to fulfil mandatory military service (conscription) in another state. Should the absence be for up to twelve consecutive months, it may be justified only if serious reasons can be shown; these can be pregnancy and maternity, serious illness, studies, and so on. After the right to permanent residence has been obtained, it may only be lost if the person concerned has been absent from Greece for more than two consecutive years.

*98.* It should be noted that, in practice, it is rather difficult to prove long periods of absence from Greece given that the entry and the departure of these categories of foreigners are not recorded within the Schengen area. Thus, Article 4 of Presidential Decree 106/2007 stipulates that this category of persons, which enjoys preferential treatment, has the right to leave the Greek territory to go to another Member

172. Presidential Decree 106/2007, Free movement and residence in the Greek territory of the citizens of the European Union and the members of their families, FEK 2007 Issue A' No. 135.

State and that no exit visa or other equivalent document shall be required. Equally, Article 5(2) thereof provides that the possession of a valid residence card of a family member of an EU citizen exempts those family members who are third-country nationals from the obligation to have an entry visa for Greece. When EU citizens and their family members, who are also EU citizens, enter for the first time the Greek territory, they enjoy the right to stay for a period of up to three months without any conditions or formalities, provided that they hold a valid national identity card or a valid (i.e., not expired) passport. As regards the family members of an EU citizen, who are nationals of a third (non-EU) state, they also have the right to stay in Greece for a period of up to three months without any conditions or formalities, subject to two conditions: they hold a valid passport or a visa (in those cases where a visa is required) and they accompany an EU citizen or enter the Greek Territory to meet an EU citizen. It follows that, in accordance with the rules of EU law, the residence of the members of the family of an EU citizen, regardless of their nationality, is completely intertwined with the residence of the EU citizen himself. And it will last for as long as the EU citizen in question maintains the conditions and requirements for lawful residence in the Member State concerned.

*99.* There is, however, a restriction in the exercise and enjoyment of the above right: under Article 6(3) of Presidential Decree 106/2007, it will be applied provided that the EU citizens and family members do not constitute an excessive burden on the social welfare system of Greece. What constitutes 'excessive burden' is not defined therein and no doubt differentiates from case to case and according to the personal circumstances of the persons in question. As far as Directive 2004/38 is concerned, it refers to the notion of 'unreasonable burden' but again no definition has been given. In the context of EU law, when questions of interpretation come up, given the necessity that the relevant rules of EU law must be applied in a uniform manner across all Member States, it is the duty of the CJEU to rule authoritatively on the precise meaning and content of legal provisions, notions, etc. In most cases, the CJEU does so when national courts, by taking advantage of a specific kind of proceedings, the so-called reference for a preliminary ruling,[173] put to it exactly such questions of interpretation.

*100.* Regarding Directive 2004/38 and the requirement that EU citizens and their family members do not become an unreasonable burden on the host country's social welfare system, the CJEU has made several judgments. Suffice to mention two of them. In the first relevant judgment, the CJEU held that EU law precludes 'legislation of a Member State which permits the authorities of that Member State to refuse to grant a social assistance benefit to a direct relative in the ascending line who, at the time the application for that benefit is made, is dependent on a worker who is a Union citizen … on the ground that the grant of the said benefit would have the effect that that family member would no longer be dependent on the worker who is a Union citizen and would thus become an unreasonable burden on the social

173. *See* Art. 267 TFEU and Art. 19 TEU; Arts 93 to 118 of the Rules of Procedure of the CJEU; and CJEU, Recommendations to national courts and tribunals in relation to the initiation of preliminary ruling proceedings, O.J. C 380, 8.11.2019, p. 1, which have been applied since 8 Nov. 2019.

assistance system of the said Member State'.[174] In the second relevant judgment, it held that '[it] must be interpreted as meaning that a Union citizen minor has sufficient resources not to become an unreasonable burden on the social assistance system of the host Member State during his period of residence, despite his resources being derived from income obtained from the unlawful employment of his father, a third-country national without a residence card and work permit'.[175]

174. *See* CJEU, Case C-488/21, *GV v. Chief Appeals Officer and Others*, Judgment, 21 Dec. 2023, ECLI:EU:C:2023:1013.
175. *See* CJEU, Case C-93/18, *Ermira Bajratari v. Secretary of State for the Home Department*, Judgment, 2 Oct. 2019, ECLI:EU:C:2019:809.

# Chapter 2. Economic Migration

## §1. Employment

### I. Conditions

*101.* The practical aspects of the process of immigration for the purpose of employment have been regulated by EU law. The relevant EU legal instrument is Directive 2011/98.[176] There are two principal themes in this legal regime. The first is that the EU has decided in favour of issuing foreigners a single permit that covers both their residence and access to employment. It is no longer possible to issue separate permits for residence and for work. The second is that 'third country workers' (a term that is, for all practical means and purposes, equivalent to 'migrant workers'), who are legally residing in the territory of a Member State, are entitled to certain rights that must be common across the EU.

*102.* The provisions of Directive 2011/98 have been incorporated into the Greek legal order in Chapter III of Part C of Law 5038/2023 (Articles 80–82). According to Article 81(1), its ambit covers two categories of third-country nationals: (a) those who apply for the first time to be issued a residence permit for the purpose of work; and (b) those who enter or who have already been accepted into the Greek territory pursuant to another provision of Law 5038/2023 stipulating the issuance of a residence permit envisaging the right to work. However, there are twelve categories of third-country nationals, who do not come under the ambit of these provisions. They include, *inter alia*, the following categories: (a) family members of EU citizens who have exercised the right of free movement within the EU, in accordance with the provisions of the aforementioned Presidential Decree 106/2007; (b) third-country nationals, who together with members of their family, regardless of nationality, enjoy free movement rights, which are equivalent to those of EU citizens, by virtue of agreements concluded between the EU and the Member States or between the EU and third countries; (c) persons who have applied for admission or have been admitted to the Greek territory as seasonal workers, in accordance with Articles 63–65 of Law 5038/2023 (examined *infra*); (d) persons who have submitted an application for admission or have been admitted to the Greek territory as self-employed workers or happen to be holders of residence permits for investment purposes, in accordance with Articles 96–100 of Law 5038/2023; and (e) third-country nationals, who are allowed to work on the basis of a national entry visa, in accordance with Articles 68–79 of Law 5038/2023.[177]

---

176. Directive 2011/98/EU of the European Parliament and of the Council of 13 Dec. 2011 on a single application procedure for a single permit for third-country nationals to reside and work in the territory of a Member State and on a common set of rights for third-country workers legally residing in a Member State, O.J. L 343, 23.12.2011, p. 1.

177. These categories cover the following persons: digital nomads (residence title type Z.1, stipulated in Art. 68 of Law 5038/2023, *see supra*); members of artistic groups (residence title Type Z.2, Art. 69 thereof); intellectual creators, including writers, directors, painters, sculptors, actors, musicians,

*103.* According to Article 81(3) of Law 5038/2023, the single residence permit is issued or renewed in accordance with the rules and procedures which are laid down in Articles 10 and 11 of Law 5038/2023. The whole process must be completed within four months from the day the application was submitted unless the competent public authority believes that additional supporting documents ought to be produced, in which case the process is suspended for as long as the third-country national has not produced them. Only in exceptional cases that have to do with the complexity of the application could the single residence permit be issued with an extension of a maximum of three months, i.e., a total of seven months. In case these strict deadlines are not observed, the Immigration Code does not stipulate what the consequences will be but refers, on the one hand, to Article 4 and to Article 10 of the aforementioned Code of Administrative Procedures[178] and, on the other hand, to Article 45 of Presidential Decree 18/1989.[179] In a nutshell, these provisions provide the following: (a) in cases of force majeure, a public authority acts lawfully even if it has not observed the deadlines envisaged in the relevant legislation; (b) if the stipulated deadlines have not been met, the applicant is entitled to seek and receive compensation; and (c) an action for annulment brought against a public authority on the grounds of abuse of authority or breach of law is only allowed against acts issued by administrative authorities, which are not subject to any other legal remedy before a court of justice.

*104.* Third-country nationals working in Greece and having as legal title the single residence and work permit enjoy equal treatment with Greek nationals. This

singers, choreographers, etc. (residence title Type Z.3, Art. 70); third-country nationals being transferred by a company which has been established in an EU Member State or in the EEA for the purpose of providing their services (residence title Type Z.4, Art. 71); third-country nationals being transferred from a company which has been established in a third country for the purpose of providing their services (residence title type Z.5, Art. 72); leaders of organized tourist groups (residence title Type Z.6, Art. 73); athletes, coaches and other qualified personnel who accompany the athletes for practise and who will participated in international sports events (residence title Type Z.7, Art. 74); third-country nationals who are students in tertiary education and are involved in remunerated internship programmes (residence title Type Z.8, Art. 75); Australian nationals entering Greece as participants in the programme for youth mobility, pursuant to the Memorandum of Understanding between Greece and Australia (Work and Holiday Visa), which was signed in Canberra, Australia, on 14 May 2014, ratified by Law 4353/2015, FEK 2015 Issue A' No. 173 (residence title Type Z.9, Art. 76); fire fight personnel as well as technical and administrative staff entering Greece for forest fire fighting (residence title Type Z.10, Art. 77); third-country nationals entering Greece as scholarship holders of the American Educational Foundation of Greece (Fulbright Foundation) pursuant to the Agreement of 23 Apr. 1948 between the Hellenic Government and the Government of the United States of America, which was ratified by Law 3152/1955, FEK 1955 Issue A' No. 64, and the Convention of 22 Apr. 1980 between the Hellenic Republic and the United States of America, which was ratified by Law 1982/1991, FEK 1991 Issue A' No. 188 (residence title Type Z.11, Art. 78); and third-country nationals, who have applied to be admitted to study in Greece or to get acquainted with the life in *Ageion Oros* (Mount Athos) or to get acquainted with solitary life and monasticism in Greece (residence title Type Z.12, Art. 79). *See also* the Appendix to the present monograph (List of the categories and types of residence permits).

178. Law 2690/1999, as last amended by Law 4962/2022, *supra*.

179. Presidential Decree 18/1989, Codification of the legislation provisions on the Council of State, FEK 1989 Issue A' No. 8.

is expressly stated in Article 82 of Law 5038/2023. In particular, the right to equal treatment concerns the following matters, issues and aspects of employment:

a. the right to enter and reside in the Greek territory as well as the right of unhindered access to it, subject to the limitations that are envisaged in Article 176(24);[180]
b. the right to carry out the specific activity for which an entry visa to Greece has been issued;
c. the terms of employment (including the minimum age limit for work),[181] working conditions (including remuneration and dismissal), working hours, annual leave and holidays, as well as health and safety in the workplace;[182]
d. the right to strike and to undertake trade union action, the freedom of association, the freedom of joining and participating in an organization of workers or of employers or in any professional organization. Moreover, this right includes enjoying the benefits that are provided by these organizations, for example, the right to negotiate and to conclude collective employment agreements. These rights are subject to the restrictions imposed for the protection of public order and public security;
e. access to education and to vocational training;
f. the recognition of diplomas, certificates and other professional qualifications, according to the relevant national procedures;[183]

---

180. It reads: 'By virtue of a joint decision of the Ministers of Citizen Protection, Foreign Affairs, National Defense, Internal Affairs as well as Immigration and Asylum and for reasons of public interest, third-country nationals, who are in lawful residence, may be prohibited to stay or to settle in certain geographic areas of the country for the purposes of paragraph 1 of Article 18 [of Law 5038/2023].'
181. The minimum age for work in Greece is 15 years. However, minors need to have the consent of their parents or of their legal guardians to be legally employed. If consent is not given, minors are allowed to file an application to the competent court of justice and ask it to grant the necessary permission to be employed.
182. Note that the application of the labour legislation, the safeguarding of labour rights as well as the supervision of the safety and health of workers has been entrusted to the Hellenic Labour Inspectorate, an independent administrative authority, *see* Law 4808/2021, On the protection of work – Establishment of the independent administrative authority 'Labour Inspectorate' – Ratification of Convention No. 190 concerning the elimination of violence and harassment in the world of work of the International Labour Organization – Ratification of Convention No. 187 concerning the promotional framework for occupational safety and health of the International Labour Organization – Incorporation of Directive (EU) 2019/1158 of the European Parliament and of the Council of 20 Jun. 2019 on work-life balance, other provisions of the Ministry of Labour and Social Security and other emergency provisions, FEK 2021 Issue A' No. 101. The incorporated EU instruments was Directive (EU) 2019/1158 of the European Parliament and of the Council of 20 Jun. 2019 on work-life balance for parents and carers and repealing Council Directive 2010/18/EU, O.J. L 188, 12.7.2019, p. 79.
183. The Hellenic National Academic Recognition and Information Center is the official body for the academic recognition of titles and qualifications awarded by foreign higher education institutions, *see* Arts 297–316, 442–444 and 479–481 of Law 4957/2022, New Horizons in Higher Education Institutions: Strengthening the quality, functionality and connection of Higher Education Institutions with society, and other provisions, FEK 2022 Issue A' No. 141.

g. national legislation concerning social security systems;[184]
h. without prejudice to existing bilateral agreements, the payment of amounts relating to the so-called acquisitions rights under statutory old-age pensions as provided for in the national legislation or in the legislation of other EU Member States that owe the amounts in question when a third-country national has moved to a third country;[185]
i. access to goods and services that are made available to the public, including the acquisition of housing, as well as access to services provided by job search companies; and
j. tax benefits, provided that the migrant worker is considered to have his tax residence in Greece.

*105.* It should be noted that Article 82(4) of Law 5038/2023 clarifies that the right to equal treatment is without prejudice to the right of the competent public authorities to reject or revoke any residence permit that has been issued pursuant to the provisions of the Immigration Code.

## II. Procedures

*106.* Regarding the procedural aspects of having a residence and work permit issued, Article 3 of the aforementioned Joint Ministerial Decision 95391/2024 stipulates that a national entry visa (the so-called Visa D) and a residence permit for dependent employment[186] and for seasonal work (Category 'E' permit) may be granted by the relevant Greek diplomatic or consular authority, once it has received the decision of the competent authority in Greece approving the employment of a third-country national to a specific employer, who must have already signed an

184. *See* further, Regulation (EC) 883/2004 of the European Parliament and of the Council of 29 Apr. 2004 on the coordination of social security systems, O.J. L 166, 30.4.2004, p. 1, as last amended by Regulation (EU) 2019/1149 of the European Parliament and of the Council of 20 Jun. 2019 establishing a European Labour Authority, amending Regulations (EC) No. 883/2004, (EU) No. 492/2011, and (EU) 2016/589 and repealing Decision (EU) 2016/344, O.J. L 186, 11.7.2019, p. 21.
185. *See* I. Katsaroumpas, 'Greece' in V. Bogoeski and Z. Rasnača (eds), *Report on the Social Security Rights of Short-Term Third-Country National Migrant Workers*, European Trade Union Institute, Report 2023.04, Brussels, 2023, 67–70.
186. The term 'dependent employment' is not defined in the Immigration Code. However, in Greek labour law it means the agreement between an employer and an employee, under which the employee undertakes the main obligation to provide his work to the employer, under his supervision and control, while the main obligation of the employer is to pay the agreed salary to the employee. The criterion that characterizes an agreement as a contract of dependent employment and not as another form of labour is that the relationship between employer and employee is founded on personal dependence. The latter is manifested by the right of the employer to give instructions to the employee as regards the way, the place and the time of the provision of his work as well as to exercise supervision over the employee and to control whether he complies with his instructions. The other forms are primarily the contract for the performance of a work (i.e., one person (contractor) undertakes towards a third person (employer/client) the obligation to carry out a certain work in return for receiving the agreed remuneration), and the contract for the provision of independent services (i.e., a provider of independent services undertakes to provide specific work to a third person (client/contractual partner) without being subject to his supervision and control and without being restricted as regards the way, the place and the time of the provision of his services).

employment contract. The latter may concern dependent employment or highly qualified employment, or seasonal employment.[187]

*107.* In particular, residence permit type E1 concerns highly qualified employment, which will be offered by a third-country national to an employer who is based in Greece.[188] This resident permit is better known as the 'EU Blue Card'. It is presently regulated under the aforementioned EU Directive 2021/1883, and concerns third-country nationals, who are deemed to be highly qualified and possess higher level professional skills. The latter have been defined in Article 4 of Law 3058/2023 according to whether they relate to specific occupations or not. Thus, in respect of occupations concerning Information and Communications Technology Services Managers (International Standard Classification of Occupation (ISCO)-08 classification 133)[189] and Information and Communications Technology Professionals (ISCO-08 classification 25), third-country nationals must possess knowledge, skills and abilities that are certified by professional experience, which has been acquired during a period of at least three years within a period of seven years immediately before applying for the 'EU Blue Card', and at a level corresponding to a higher education degree that is relevant to the third-country national's occupation (as his occupation is specified in the employment contract). And in respect of other occupations, third-country nationals must possess, only if it is provided for by Greek law, knowledge, skills and abilities which are certified with professional experience of at least five years and at a level corresponding to a higher education degree relevant to the occupation (as specified in the employment contract).

*108.* Pursuant to Article 4 of Joint Ministerial Decision 95391/2024, the process for being granted an 'EU Blue Card' is divided into three consecutive stages. During the first stage, the competent national authorities approve that the third-country national is able to perform the highly skilled employment stated in the employment contract. During the second stage, the third-country national will be issued with a national entry visa. And during the third stage, he will be granted the relevant residence permit and, hence, he will be in possession of the 'EU Blue Card'.

---

187. Residence permits for the provision of dependent employment are further divided in Types E1, E2, E3, E4, E5 and E6.

188. The nationality of the employer is of no relevance: he may be a Greek national, a national of another EU Member State or a foreigner. Equally, if the employer is a legal person, it can be a company that is owned by Greek interests or owned by foreign interests, e.g., a branch or a subsidiary of a multinational enterprise. *See also* Joint Ministerial Decision 225679/2024, Determination of the amount and ways of proving the availability of sufficient resources provided for in the provisions of Law 5038/2023 and in other regulations, as well as the amount and ways of proving the required income for the application of the provisions of Arts 84 and 144 of Law 5038/2023, FEK 2024, Issue B' No. 5223.

189. ISCO is a four-level classification of occupation groups, which has been devised and is managed by the International Labour Organization, *see* ILO, International Standard Classification of Occupations, ISCO-08. Structure, Group Definitions and Correspondence Tables, International Labour Office, Geneva, 2012, at: https://www.ilo.org/publications/international-standard-classification-occupations-2008-isco-08-structure. Further, *see* Commission Recommendation of 29 Oct. 2009 on the use of the International Standard Classification of Occupations (ISCO-08), O.J. L 292, 10.11.2009, p. 31.

*109.* For the first stage to be completed, the prospective employer must submit an application to the competent Greek authority accompanied by, *inter alia,* the following supporting documents. The first document is the employment contract. It must specifically show that the work to be done concerns highly qualified employment, which will be offered in Greece and for a period of at least six months. The third-country national (i.e., the employee) must be remunerated with a gross annual salary which is not lower than the national minimum wage for highly qualified employment in Greece. Article 31(1) of Law 5038/2023 has set the latter at 1.6 times (under the previous Immigration and Social Integration Code it was 1.5 times) the amount of the average gross annual salary in Greece.[190] Regarding the second document, if the profession of the third-country national/employee is regulated by the Greek legislation, it will take the form of an attestation/certificate, which will be issued by the Council for the Recognition of Professional Qualifications and will show that the requirements of Presidential Decree 38/2010 vis-a-vis the exercise of the profession specified in the employment contract are met.[191] However, if the third-country national's profession is unregulated under Greek law, documents must be produced showing that he possesses the high professional qualifications, which are needed to perform the employment in question.

*110.* As regards the national entry visa, over and above the approval of the highly qualified employment (namely, the aforementioned first stage), the necessary conditions are that the employee has signed the employment contract, that the general supporting documents laid down in the Ministerial Decision issued under the authority of Article 176(8) of Law 5038/2023 have been submitted and that a consular fee of EUR 180 has been paid to obtain the visa. Finally, the issuance of the residence permit will require the following documents: the national entry visa, the signed contract for highly qualified employment, the announcement to the competent public authority that the third-country national has been recruited, a confirmation that an application has been filed with the relevant public social security scheme for the third-country national to obtain full insurance for illness and for all other risks that Greek nationals are covered. The cost of obtaining the residence permit has also been set at EUR 150.

*111.* Setting the maximum number of third-country nationals, who will be accepted in Greece to carry out paid employment (including seasonal employment) is a government decision. This is stipulated in Article 26(1) of the Immigration

---

190. According to data by the Ministry of Labour and Social Security, for the year 2023 the average monthly salary was EUR 1,251, while for the year 2022 it stood at EUR 1,176.

191. Presidential Decree 38/2010 on the adaptation of the Greek legislation to Directive 2005/36/EC regarding the recognition of professional qualifications, FEK 2010 Issue A' No. 78. *See* further, Directive 2005/36/EC of the European Parliament and of the Council of 7 Sep. 2005 on the recognition of professional qualifications, O.J. L 255, 30.9.2005, p. 22, as presently in force following the adoption of Directive 2024/505 of the European Parliament and of the Council of 7 Feb. 2024 amending Directive 2005/36/EC as regards the recognition of professional qualifications of nurses responsible for general care trained in Romania, O.J. L, 2024/505, 12.2.2024. Note that under Art. 2 of Directive 2024/505, Member States must bring into force their domestic laws, regulations and administrative provisions necessary to comply with it by 4 Mar. 2025.

Code, which provides that an act of the Council of Ministers shall be issued during the last quarter of each year, upon the recommendation of the Minister of Labour and Social Affairs. This act shall determine for the following year the maximum number of positions that will be made available for third-country nationals to be engaged in dependent employment as well as in seasonal work.

*112.* It should be noted that only recently were the provisions of labour law codified into a single legal instrument.[192] As regards the connection between labour law and immigration, Article 15 of Presidential Decree 80/2022 stipulates that labour law promotes the principle of equal treatment while combating discrimination on the grounds of: (a) race, colour, national or ethnic origin, and descent, in accordance with the aforementioned EU Directive 2000/43;[193] and (b) religion, disability or chronic disease, age, marital or social status, sexual orientation, gender identity, etc., in accordance with the aforementioned EU Directive 2000/78.[194] Article 17(1) of Presidential Decree 80/2022 provides that the principle of equal treatment, which does not take into account, *inter alia*, national or ethnic origin, shall apply to all persons, in the public and private sectors, in relation to the following matters: conditions of access to employment and employment in general; access to all types and levels of vocational training and retraining; conditions of work and employment, in particular as regards remuneration, dismissal, health and safety at work; and membership in a workers' trade union.

*113.* In addition, under the second paragraph of Article 17, the same principle of equal treatment shall apply to all persons, irrespective of whether they are employed in the public sector or in the private sector, as regards the following matter: social protection, including social security and health care; social benefits and tax concessions or advantages; education; and access to the supply of goods and services that are generally made available to the public, including housing. Finally, Article 17(3) states that the principle of equal treatment shall not apply where a difference of treatment based on nationality is specifically justified and is without prejudice to the provisions on the legal status of third-country nationals outside the EU or stateless persons who live in Greece.

*114.* According to Article 28(1) of Presidential Decree 80/2022, the entity that is responsible for monitoring and promoting the implementation of the principle of equal treatment in the private and public sectors irrespective of race, colour, national

192. *See* Presidential Decree 80/2022, Code of Individual Labour Law, FEK 2022 Issue A' No. 222, as last amended by Law 5089/2024, Equality in civil marriage, amendment of the Civil Code and other provisions, FEK 2024 Issue A' No. 27.

193. Council Directive 2000/43/EC of 29 Jun. 2000 implementing the principle of equal treatment between persons irrespective of racial or ethnic origin; it was transposed into Greek law under Law 4443/2016, *supra*.

194. Council Directive 2000/78/EC of 27 Nov. 2000 establishing a general framework for equal treatment in employment and occupation, O.J. L 303, 2.12.2000, p. 16; it was transposed into Greek law under Law 4443/2016, *supra*.

or ethnic origin, descent, etc., is the Greek Ombudsman.[195] Moreover, in pursuance to the provisions of Article 29 thereof, there are other public sector entities and bodies which are entrusted with functions as regards equal treatment and non-discrimination. In particular: (a) the so-called independent authorities[196] are entrusted with the implementation and promotion of the principle of equal treatment regardless of race, colour, national or ethnic origin, etc., and in accordance with the purposes and provisions of Presidential Decree 80/2022; (b) the General Secretariat of Justice and Human Rights of the Ministry of Justice, as part of its responsibilities for the protection of human rights and the elimination of all forms of discrimination, must ensure the promotion of the principle of equal treatment; (c) the Department of Social Inclusion and Social Cohesion of the Ministry of Labour and Social Affairs, in exercising its mandate, is obligated to monitor the implementation of anti-discrimination policies in the field of employment and in workplaces and must ensure that employees and employers are informed and be made aware of non-discrimination in the workplace; and (d) the Directorate of Immigration Policy of the Ministry of the Interior is also mandated to contribute to the promotion of the principle of equal treatment.

*115.* Interestingly enough, Article 29 of Presidential Decree 80/2022 does not lay down any obligations for the Ministry of Migration and Asylum, even though it is evident that the principle of equal treatment and the prohibition of discrimination should in principle apply to migrant workers as well. Finally, Article 32 of Presidential Decree 80/2022 contains the following saving clause: 'The [above] provisions [shall] not affect more favourable provisions regarding the promotion and observance of the principle of equal treatment and shall not be a reason to reduce the existing level of the protection provided.'

*116.* It should also be noted that several states have concluded agreements with the EU on the basis of which their nationals, who are working legally in an EU Member State, are entitled to the same working conditions as the nationals of their host country. These states are (broken down according to region): Algeria, Morocco, and Tunisia; the Russian Federation and Ukraine; Albania, Montenegro, North Macedonia, Bosnia and Herzegovina, Kosovo and Serbia; Andorra and San Marino; and the seventy-nine countries of the so-called African, Caribbean and Pacific Group of State's, now known as the Organization of African, Caribbean and Pacific States.[197] It follows that as regards the nationals of other countries, the right to work

195. The Office of the Ombudsman is regulated pursuant to Law 3094/2003, The Ombudsman and other provisions, FEK 2003 Issue A' No. 10, as amended and presently in force.

196. These are administrative bodies, which are part of the legal entity of the Greek State, enjoy administrative independence and autonomy and also have financial autonomy. Some of these 'independent authorities' have a constitutional foundation, in the sense that the Constitution expressly mentions their existence and their activities (namely, the Hellenic Authority for Communication Security and Privacy, the Supreme Council for Civil Personnel Selection, the Greek Ombudsman and the National Council for Radio and Television), while some 'independent authorities' also operate as national regulatory authorities (NRAs).

197. For the list of countries, *see* https://www.oacps.org/about-us/.

in an EU Member State principally depends on the legislation of the host Member State.[198] The obvious exception is if the third-country nationals happen to be members of the family of an EU national.

*117.* To return to the act of the Council of Ministers, the Code of Immigration stipulates that the setting of the maximum annual number of migrant workers to enter Greece will be calculated by taking into account the employment needs that Greece will have during the following year. The maximum number is given as a whole and then it is broken down into the thirteen Regions of Greece according to the different categories/types of employment. The latter are determined on the basis of European Skills, Competences, Qualifications and Occupations (ESCO), which stands for ESCO.[199] The number of positions per employment category is allowed to be increased by a maximum of 10% to cover unforeseen and extraordinary events (force majeure situations).

*118.* As regards the specific manner through which the annual number of incoming migrant workers will be set, Article 26(2) of the Immigration Code stipulates that once every year the Ministry of Labour and Social Affairs shall consult with the Economic and Social Committee of Greece (ESC)[200] as well as with the Public Employment Service (DYPA)[201] on the short term and medium-term prospects of the Greek economy, and shall take into account several parameters, including the level of employment offer from Greek nationals, from nationals of other EU Member States and from third-country nationals legally residing in the country; the rate of unemployment; and the number of migrant workers who had been recalled in previous years.[202]

---

198. Note that special arrangements may be in place with specific third states, but these cannot be discussed in the context of the present monograph. Suffice to give the example of Switzerland, *see* Agreement between the European Community and its Member States, of the one part, and the Swiss Confederation, of the other, on the free movement of persons, signed on 21 Jun. 1999, entered into force 1 Jun. 2002, O.J. L 114, 30.4.2002, p. 6.
199. This is a European Commission project providing descriptions of more than 3,000 occupations and of some 14,000 skills in the 28 languages used in the EU. Note that ESCO's aim has actually to do with intra-EU migration, not with immigration towards EU Member States. More specifically, ESCO is meant to support job mobility across the EU by making the labour market more integrated and more efficient by offering a 'common language' on the different occupations and skills.
200. The Economic and Social Committee was established pursuant to Law 2232/1994. Its structure and activities are modelled on the European Economic and Social Council, one of the organs of the EU. Since 2001, The Economic and Social Committee has received constitutional recognition: under Art. 82(3) of the Constitution its mission is to conduct the social dialogue on the general policy of Greece and, in particular, on the directions that the economic policy and the social policy should have as well as to formulate opinions on draft laws and on legislative proposals that have been referred to it.
201. Despite its name, DYPA is not about employment in the public sector but primarily for the private sector. It was originally established in the early 1970s and took its present form under Law 4921/2022, Jobs Again: Reorganization of the Public Employment Service (GPES) and digitalization of its services, enhancement of the skills of the labour force and diagnosis of the work needs and other provisions, FEK 2022 Issue A' No. 75.
202. In Art. 4 of Law 5038/2023, the 'recall' of a migrant worker has been defined as the procedure by virtue of which it is possible for a third-country national to enter and stay in Greece for the purpose of offering dependent employment to a specific employer and for a specific type of occupation.

*119.* Of direct relevance is Article 27 of the Immigration Code, which is titled 'Regulation of issues relating to the admission process of third-country nationals for the provision of employment'. Under the first paragraph of Article 27, any Greek employer, who wishes to hire migrant workers for the provision of dependent employment, must apply through the electronic services of the Ministry of Migration and Asylum, and must indicate the number of jobs, the personal details and nationality of third-country nationals to be employed, the category of employment as well as the period (length) of employment. The application must be accompanied by the documents which are set out in the aforementioned Ministerial Decision No. 95391/2024 in conjunction with Ministerial Decision 133226/2024.[203] It follows that the third-country nationals in question will be issued with an entry visa for dependent employment. In the case of migrant workers to be recalled (residence permit Type 'E.4'), Article 27 should be read in conjunction with Article 61 of the Immigration Code. It provides that the prospective employer in Greece must accompany the application with: (a) a copy of a valid employment contract whose duration is for at least one year and from which it derives that the migrant worker will receive a remuneration which will be at least equal to the monthly wages of an unskilled worker;[204] and (b) a copy of his annual tax return or other document proving his ability to pay in full the salary of the recalled migrant worker/s. The fee for the examination of application is EUR 200 for every third-country national.

*120.* Under the previous legislative regime (Law 4251/2014, Code of Immigration and Social Integration), the maximum number of migrant workers allowed to enter Greece was set out in a joint ministerial decision, which had to be issued six months before the beginning of a two year period by the Minister of Immigration and Asylum, the Minister for Development and Investment, the Minister of Foreign Affairs, the Minister for Labour and Social Affairs, the Minister of Shipping and Islands Policy, and the Minister of Rural Development and Food (previously, the Ministry of Agriculture). Therefore, the relevant decision for the years 2023 and 2024 ought to have been issued before July 2022 but it was actually issued in early April 2023.[205] That this deadline was not observed was a common occurrence.

*121.* Arguably, it signified the inability of the Greek public authorities to plan ahead and to feel obliged to follow the strict deadlines that are imposed by the legislation. It should be noted that the Greek legislation does not envisage any specific penalties if the competent public authorities fail to observe deadlines; this has contributed to an ethos of impunity which is widespread across the country. According to Joint Ministerial Decision No. 35400/2023, the maximum number of migrant

203. Joint Ministerial Decision 133226/2024, Determination of the documents relating to the first paragraph of Art. 27 of Law 5038/2023, FEK 2024 Issue B' No. 26.

204. It follows that the Immigration Code ensures the equality of minimum wages to be paid to migrant workers and to non-third-country nationals' workers.

205. Joint Ministerial Decision No. 35400/2023, Determination of the maximum number of residence permits for the employment of third-country nationals for the years 2023 and 2024, FEK 2023 Issue B' No. 2189.

workers for the years 2023 and 2024 has been set at was set at 167,925 third-country nationals. This figure covered the following types of employment/ occupations: dependent employment, seasonal employment, fishermen, and highly skilled employment. On 1 March 2024, the Decision was amended by Joint Ministerial Decision No. 14761/2024.[206]

*122.* For purposes of illustration and to give an indication of its content, reference will be made to some of the occupations for which the issuance of residence permits is envisaged in the amended Decision in five different Regions, namely the Region of Attica (it includes the capital city, Athens), the Region of Central Macedonia (it includes the second-largest city, Thessaloniki), the Region of the Peloponnese, the Region of the Ionian Islands (a Region that comprises only islands) and the Region of Western Hellas. In particular, for the Region of Attica, the amended Ministerial Decision envisaged a total number of 9,967 residence permits for the years 2023 and 2024. This figure included: 100 permits for 'high skilled employment Directive 2009/50/EC' of which 20 permits for 'high skilled employment Directive 2009/50/EC (professional divers)', 2,320 permits for seasonal workers, 2,500 permits for caregivers of persons with disabilities and caregivers for the elderly, 2,000 permits for construction workers, and 180 permits for ship painters and sandblasting machine operators. As regards the Region of Central Macedonia, a total of 6,125 residence permits is envisaged that include, among others: 1,310 permits for dependent employment, 800 permits for unskilled agricultural, livestock, forestry and fishing workers, 3 permits for computer programmers, 4,015 permits for seasonal employment (of which 4,000 permits for unskilled agricultural, livestock, forestry and fishing workers and 15 permits for kitchen support staff), 10 permits for forklift operators, and 50 permits for cleaners. For the Region of the Peloponnese only 10 residence permits are envisaged, and these are for 'highly skilled workers Directive 2009/50/EC (recreational scuba diving instructors)', while for the Region of the Ionian Islands, there were 70 residence permits allocated, of which 45 permits for dependent employment and restaurant vendors, and 35 permits for kitchen staff. Finally, 2,225 residence permits for only permanent employment were allocated to the Region of Western Hellas, which included, among others: 50 permits for workers in the food industry, 10 permits for workers operating sheet folding machines, 50 permits for caregivers of persons with disabilities and caregivers for the elderly, 20 permits for workers who package and store agricultural products, and 5 permits for restaurant waiters.

## III. Duration and Loss

*123.* According to Article 13 of Law 5038/2023, the duration of the initial residence permit is three years, and it is always possible to renew it for the same period

206. Joint Ministerial Decision No. 14761/2024, Amendment of Joint Ministerial Decision No. 35400/03-04-2023 'Determination of the maximum number of residence permits for the employment of third-country nationals for the years 2023 and 2024', FEK 2024 Issue B' No. 1390.

of time. Specific provisions apply to the aforementioned 'EU Blue Cards'. In particular, Article 34(2) provides that they are valid for two years and if the employment contract with less than two years duration, then it will be valid for the duration of the contract plus three months. However, if the passport of the holder of an 'EU Blue Card' expires before the last day of the 'EU Blue Card' validity, the latter shall be valid until the day of the passport's expiration.

*124.* While an 'EU Blue Card' is relatively easily granted, provided of course that the relevant conditions have been met, there are many reasons and grounds for which it may not be renewed or withdrawn. Thus, Article 35 sets out, among others, the following eight instances:

a. where the 'EU Blue Card' or the documents that the third-country nationals submitted to be granted it were fraudulently obtained, forged, or otherwise tampered with. Presumably, the third-country nationals concerned should also be criminally prosecuted, but the Immigration Code is silent on the criminal aspects of the illegally obtained 'EU Blue Card';
b. when the third-country citizen concerned no longer has a valid employment contract for highly skilled employment or the qualifications which are necessary for being regarded as capable of working in highly skilled employment. However, *see* later under h. which envisages that the holder of an 'EU Blue Card' may remain in Greece while being unemployed;
c. when the salary of the third-country citizen concerned no longer meets the minimum salary criteria, as has already been explained (Article 31(1) of Law 5038/2023);
d. for reasons of public order and public security;
e. where the employer does not fulfil his legal obligations regarding social insurance, taxation, labour rights or working conditions. It is not clear why in this instance the 'EU Blue Card' holder should be 'penalized' by not renewing or revoking it;
f. when the 'EU Blue Card' holder does not have sufficient resources for his own maintenance and/or for the maintenance of his family members without having to resort to the social welfare system of Greece. The competent authorities will assess the adequacy of resources on the basis of their nature and regularity and will also take into account the national minimum salary, the number of family members as well as any contributions that family members make to the household income;
g. when the 'EU Blue Card' holder resides in the Greek territory for purposes other than those for which he was granted residence; and
h. when the 'EU Blue Card' holder has not complied with the procedures and the requirements laid down in Article (2)–(4) of Law 40 of 5038/2023. Briefly, these provisions state that Blue Card holders are obliged to notify the Directorate of Residence Permits of the Ministry of Immigration and Asylum of the change of employer or any other change that could affect the fulfilment of the criteria on the basis of which he was admitted to Greece (Article 31 of 5038/2023). They must also notify the Directorate without delay, of the start and, if relevant, the end of the unemployment period, during which they are entitled to seek other

employment. Presumably, the holder of the 'EU Blue Card' must look not for any employment, but for highly skilled employment. Even though not expressly laid down in the Immigration Code, if he got any other employment he would no longer fulfil the basic criteria for being granted an 'EU Blue Card'.

## IV. A Special Type of Residence Permit for the Employment of Illegal Migrants (Article 193 of Law 5078/2023)

*125.* Pursuant to Article 193(1) of the aforementioned Law 5078/2023, the Secretary of the relevant Decentralized Administration will issue a residence permit bearing the right of access to employment and to the provision of services, if the applicant third-country nationals meet the following four conditions: (a) they have received an offer of employment from an employer located in Greece; (b) they had resided in Greece until 30 November 2023 without having a residence permit; (c) they have since continued to live in Greece; and (d) they had completed at least three consecutive years of residence in the country before submitting the application (this requirement must be proven with the production of appropriate documents). But the second paragraph of Article 193 adds four more conditions. First, the applicant must possess a passport, even if it has expired; however, a residence permit may still be granted if it is objectively impossible to provide the applicant with a passport. Second, the applicant poses no threat to public order and to public security. Third, a fee of EUR 316 has been paid. Fourth, the (prospective) employer has solemnly declared that he undertakes to employ the applicant (paid work or provision of services), who has already submitted an application to be granted an Article 193 residence permit.

*126.* The third paragraph of Article 193 concerns the family members of a third-country national, who has already been issued with a residence permit under Article 193(1). In particular, a residence permit will be granted to the spouse, to the parents and to the minor child/ren, provided that they had lived in Greece until 30 November 2023 and, as regards the spouse and the parents, that they are unable to be granted a residence permit according to one of the provisions of the Immigration Code. As is expected, the duration of the residence permits of family members is directly linked to that of the applicant/holder. It follows that, as these residence permits are dependent upon his permit, in case the permit is cancelled/revoked or otherwise impaired, the family members' permits will have the same fate. Pursuant to Article 193(7), this type of residence permit is an exceptional one: it shall be granted only once and have a duration of three years, at the end of which the holder will be given the opportunity to apply for a change of residence permit category in accordance with Article 12 of the Immigration Code, provided that he has an active insurance cover/policy and has fulfilled all tax obligations.

*127.* It follows that the Article 193 residence permits are a one-off opportunity for irregular migrant workers to regularize their own stay and that of their family members. The fourth paragraph of Article 193 sets out a deadline for applying, which is 31 December 2024. Applicants are given sixty days to submit (also electronically) evidence of commencement of employment (e.g., a contract), which must be specifically with the employer, who must have already submitted the aforementioned solemn declaration. Should the applicant fail to meet this deadline, his application shall be rejected. Finally, these residence permits may be revoked by the Secretary of the Decentralized Administration, in case the holder is not employed for a specific period of time. The length of time is not laid down in Article 193 but, as stipulated in Article 193(4), a joint decision of the Ministers of Immigration and Asylum, Interior, and Labour and Social Security will regulate this and all other necessary details for the implementation of these provisions.

*128.* Interestingly enough, under Article 193(9) another category of third-country nationals has come under the ambit of this special category of residence permit. Thus, third-country nationals who, before the end of December 2023, had applied for a residence permit for exceptional reasons, and their application was rejected due to non-fulfilment of the condition of seven years of continuous residence in the country, were allowed to reapply for a residence permit in accordance with the conditions of Article 193. Finally, pursuant to Article 193(11), those third-country nationals, who reside illegally in the country and do not come within the ambit of these provisions, are subject to return procedures in accordance with the relevant provisions of Law 3907/2011.[207]

## §2. Seasonal Work and Temporary Employment

*129.* Since the early 1980s, Greece has concluded a small number of bilateral agreements to regulate the seasonal work and temporary employment of migrant workers. These agreements are mostly a reflection of the fact that, at least since the early 1980s, there has been a constant shortage of labourers in two important sectors of the Greek economy, namely the agricultural and fishing sectors and the construction sector. In different epochs of the history of the Greek state, both sectors have been very important for the national economy. When it joined the EU in 1981, Greece was considered to be primarily an agricultural country with a not particularly developed industrial base. Presently, the agricultural sector employs around 400,000 people (corresponding to 10% of employment in all sectors of the economy).[208] As regards the construction sector, it is estimated that its total production value reached EUR 12.8 billion in 2023, while it is expected to reach EUR 21.4 billion by the end of 2026.[209] As regards employment, the main difference between

207. Law 3907/2011, Establishment of an Asylum Service and a First Reception Service, adaptation of Greek legislation to the provisions of Directive 2008/115/EC 'regarding the common rules and procedures in the member states for the return of illegally staying third-country nationals' and other provisions, FEK 2011 Issue A' No. 7, as last amended by the aforementioned Law 4825/2021.
208. Generally, *see* European Commission, 'Greece: Common Agricultural Policy Strategic Plan for the implementation of the CAP 2023–27', at: https://agriculture.ec.europa.eu/cap-my-country/cap-strategic-plans/greece_en.
209. Generally, *see* European Construction Industry Federation, 'Greece', at: https://fiec-statistical-report.eu/greece.

agriculture/fishing and construction is that the former sector is characterized by seasonality (hence the need for seasonal migrant workers) and is strongly affected by weather conditions, whereas the latter sector is active all year long and weather conditions may only temporarily affect it. Finally, the tourism sector is also characterized by seasonality as Greece is a popular tourist destination mostly during the summer months.

*130.* In the 1980s and the 1990s, Greece concluded three bilateral agreements with neighbouring countries that promoted the sending of migrant workers especially for seasonal or temporal employment to Greece. In chronological order, these bilateral agreements were with Egypt,[210] Bulgaria,[211] and Albania.[212] Moreover, as has already been explained, more recently, the Greek Parliament ratified bilateral seasonal migration agreements with Egypt and Bangladesh. Article 4 of Law 5038/2023 defines 'seasonal work' as the activity which is carried out in Greece for a period of up to nine months in total, per twelve-month period, in a sector of seasonal employment having a periodic character within the year. In other words, these are sectors characterized by seasonality where the level of required workforce is significantly higher. The definition given to a 'seasonal worker' is the following: the third-country national, who retains his principal place of residence in a third country, who resides legally and temporarily for reasons of employment in the Greek territory in a field of activity that depends on the change of seasons and whose work is based on one or more fixed-term employment contracts, which have been concluded directly between the third-country national and the employer who is established in Greece. There are two types of residence permits for seasonal migrant workers, residence permit Type 'E.5', which confers the right to residence and employment to the holders of a visa for the purpose of seasonal work, and residence permit Type 'E.6' which is issued to seasonal workers.

---

210. Agreement between the Hellenic Republic and the Arab Republic of Egypt for the promotion of bilateral cooperation concerning labour matters, signed in Cairo on 18 Apr. 1981, ratified by Greece under Law 1453/1984 of 14 Jun. 1984, FEK 1984 Issue A' No. 88. Further, *see* Law 1245/1982, Ratification of the Agreement between the Hellenic Republic and the Arab Republic of Egypt on exemption of Greek workers in Egypt and Egyptian workers in Greece from charges required for the granting and/or renewal of work permits signed in Cairo on 18 Apr. 1981, FEK 1982 Issue A' No. 45. To the best of one's knowledge these Agreements have never been terminated.
211. Agreement of Seasonal Employment of Labour Force between the Government of the Hellenic Republic and the Government of the Republic of Bulgaria, signed in Athens on 15 Dec. 1995, Greece ratified it under Law 2407/1996, FEK 1996 Issue A' No. 103. This Agreement lapsed when the transitional period of Bulgaria's accession to the European Union as regards Greece ended in December 2009, *see* Treaty concerning the accession of the Republic of Bulgaria and Romania to the European Union, signed on 25 Apr. 2005, entered into force on 1 Jan. 2007, O.J. L 157, 21.6.2005, p. 11. Despite the Agreement concluded in 1995, it has been argued that a large number of Bulgarian migrants entered Greece illegally, *see* E. Markova and A. Sarris, 'The Performance of Bulgarian Illegal Immigrants in the Greek Labor Market', 2 *South-Eastern Society and Politics* (1997), 57.
212. Agreement of Seasonal Employment of Labour Force between the Government of the Hellenic Republic and the Government of the Republic of Albania, signed in Athens on 17 May 1996, ratified by Greece under Law 2482/1997, FEK 1997 Issue A' No. 73.

*131.* As regards the admission of third-country nationals for the purpose of seasonal employment and, specifically, residence permits Type 'E.5', these are matters that are regulated by EU law. In particular, Chapter VI (Articles 63–65) of Law 5038/2023 transposed the provisions of the aforementioned EU Directive 2014/36 on the seasonal employment of third-country nationals into domestic law. The provisions of Chapter VI apply to third-country nationals, who either live outside the Greek territory and request that they be allowed to enter and reside in it or have already been accepted in Greece for the purpose of seasonal employment. According to the definition of 'seasonal employment' in Article 4 of Law 5038/2023, the sectors where such employment may be offered are those that are related to seasonal conditions, during which the necessary level of labour force is significantly higher than that required for normal activities.

*132.* In accordance with Article 63(7) of Law 5038/2023, Greek consular authorities decide on the application for the granting of an entry visa for the purpose of seasonal work and should communicate their decision to the applicant no later than sixty days from the day the completed application was submitted. Once third-country seasonal workers have been granted the entry visa, they must produce a certificate of family status, or a birth certificate officially translated into Greek and authenticated. This document is very important because it will be required when the request for the seasonal work residence permit is submitted when the third-country national will request a tax identification number from the Independent Authority for Public Revenue as well as a social security number from the National Social Security Fund (EFKA), the single (State) insurance fund in Greece. Seasonal workers are covered by the insurance of EFKA depending on the activity they carry out or on the nature of their employment, exactly on the same terms as Greek nationals. Finally, Article 63(10) provides that, should the validity of the entry visa for the purpose of seasonal work expire while the residence permit's examination process has not been completed, the seasonal worker concerned shall be allowed to remain in the Greek territory until the decision on the application has been taken.

*133.* As regards the issuance of the entry visa for seasonal employment, this is regulated in Article 64 of Law 5038/2023. Article 64 envisages the following three types of entry visas:

a. the national entry visa for seasonal work which has a maximum validity of nine months and allows the presence of the third-country national for nine months as well. Holders are allowed to re-enter with another seasonal employment visa only if three months have lapsed from the expiry of the previous one;
b. the national entry visa for seasonal work whose maximum period of validity period of one year and which grants the holder the right to stay for the purpose of seasonal work for up to nine months during the validity of the visa. The period of work stipulated in the migrant worker's employment contract will be taken into consideration; and

c. the uniform short-term multiple entry visa (the so-called Schengen visa) which has a maximum duration of six months and allows a stay of ninety days for seasonal work, pursuant to the provisions of the aforementioned EU Regulation 810/2009.

*134.* After completing the maximum length of stay, the seasonal migrant worker is not allowed to return to Greece if a period of three months following the completion of the seasonal employment has not lapsed. Once the period of employment has been completed, the seasonally employed third-country national must depart from the Greek territory immediately. The penalty for non-compliance is that he will not be allowed to re-enter the country for seasonal work and for a period of up to five years from the day he was obliged to depart. Naturally, this presupposes that somehow the migrant worker in question will be apprehended and repatriated to the country of origin. In reality, if he wants to remain in Greece, he will not have much trouble in becoming part of the vast black economy that has plagued the country for decades now.

*135.* Article 64(8) of Law 5038/2023 lays down the reasons why the competent Greek consular authority may decide not to grant or revoke an entry visa. These reasons include the following: the documents presented have been obtained fraudulently or have been forged; the seasonal migrant worker has submitted an application for international protection under the terms of Law 4939/2022 (*see infra*); the employer's business has been placed in liquidation; the employer does not fulfil his legal obligations regarding social security, taxation, labour rights or other conditions of employment; the third-country national has not complied with the obligations arising from a previous decision granting him an entry visa for the purpose of seasonal work; sanctions have been taken against the employer for undeclared work or illegal employment pursuant to the relevant provisions of the Immigration Code and of the aforementioned Law 4052/2012; and the third-country national is residing in Greece for purposes other than seasonal work. The third-country national has an unfettered right to be informed of the legal and factual reason on the basis of which his application (including any application for renewal) was rejected. Thus, the reasons must be notified to him. Furthermore, Article 64(10) expressly states that before reaching a decision rejecting or revoking an entry visa, the interests of the seasonal migrant worker as well as the principle of proportionality must be taken into consideration. Finally, Article 64(11) provides that if the third-country national seeks the judicial review of the rejection before an administrative court of justice, he is not released from the obligation to leave the Greek territory after the end of the maximum duration of his stay for seasonal work.

*136.* As has been mentioned *supra*, the Immigration Code was amended under Law 5130/2024, which resulted in changes and additions to the provisions of Articles 64 and 65 of Law 5038/2023. Among them, was the insertion of a new subparagraph to Article 65(1), according to which applications for the issuance of a national entry visa for seasonal employment lodged by third-country nationals, who had been granted an entry visa for seasonal work during the last five years and had complied in full with all their obligations, shall be examined as a matter of priority by the competent Greek consular offices.

*137.* Articles 63 to 65 of the Immigration Code should be regarded as *lex generalis*, while the bilateral agreements that Greece has concluded on seasonal employment with third states as *lex specialis*. A critical overview of such a bilateral agreement, the Memorandum of Understanding (MoU) between Hellas and Bangladesh on Migration and Mobility concluded in English in February 2022 (reference to it has already been made), will now be given. It should be noted that, while this a bilateral agreement, on account of the participation of Greece in the EU, there are instruments of EU law that apply to the MoU, for example, the EU-Bangladesh Standard Operating Procedures (SOPs) for the Identification and Return of Persons without an Authorization to Stay, which was signed by the European Commission and the government of Bangladesh on 20 September 2017.[213]

*138.* According to Article 3 of the MoU, its scope covers three categories of nationals of Bangladesh: (a) those who apply to be admitted to the Greek territory for temporary stay and employment in the agricultural sector as well as in other sectors that are open to seasonal employment under the Greek legislation;[214] (b) those, who at the time the MoU was signed (not at the time it entered into force), were resident in Greece and were eligible to be granted a temporary residence permit under the MoU's provisions; and (c) those who did not fulfil the conditions for entry, presence in or residence in the Greek territory. The latter category, presumably, covers those nationals of Bangladesh who were/irregularly living in the country.[215] Arguably, the MoU has three principal goals. First, to effectively legitimize the presence in Greece of thousands of/irregular nationals of Bangladesh by offering them residence permits of a five-year duration, after which period it will presumably be expected that they will return to their country of nationality. Second, to regulate the future legal flows of temporary migrant workers from Bangladesh to Greece, who are meant to stay for a maximum total period of five years and then be repatriated. Third, to fight irregular migration, migrant smuggling and trafficking in human beings (THB).

*139.* More specifically, pursuant to Article 4(2) of the MoU, during the first five years of its application, the Greek government shall grant 15,000 temporary residence permits of five-year duration to nationals of Bangladesh who, at the time of

213. Text at: https://arts.unimelb.edu.au/__data/assets/pdf_file/0009/3409830/Bangladesh-1.pdf.
214. It should be clarified that the MoU was concluded based on the provisions of the previous Immigration and Social Integration Code (Law 4251/2014), as it was in force at the time.
215. In that respect, *see* the website of the Embassy of the People's Republic of Bangladesh in Athens, '[t]he Greek side also proposed an Agreement on Readmission of undocumented Bangladeshis. Bangladesh is examining', at: https://athens.mofa.gov.bd/en/site/page/Bilateral-Relations-with-Greece. It is presumed that the MoU discussed here is the outcome of the Greek proposal.

the MoU's signing, already resided in Greece. If this provision is read together with Article 3, it transpires that it concerns primarily those nationals of Bangladesh who live in Greece/irregularly.[216]

*140.* Furthermore, the MoU provides that during the first five-year period of operation, an additional number of 4,000 temporary residence permits of a five-year duration shall be issued to nationals of Bangladesh, who apply to be admitted to Greece for temporary stay and employment in the agricultural and other sectors of the economy that are suitable for seasonal employment.[217] It follows that these 20,000 residence permits in total (4,000 per year over five years) are destined for ordinary (legal) waves of migrant temporary workers from Bangladesh to Greece. And if one adds the aforementioned 15,000 temporary residence permits, the grand total is 35,000 permits for Bangladeshis during the first five-year period.

*141.* However, the text of the MoU reveals that the figure of the 15,000 temporary residence permits for those Bangladeshis, who were already residing in Greece irregularly, was set rather arbitrarily. It also confirms the widely held opinion that the competent Greek authorities do not have a concrete idea of the number of irregular aliens in the country. This submission follows from Article 5(4) and (5), which provide that the nationals of Bangladesh must apply for these residence permits within an (exclusive) period of 180 days from the date the MoU enters into force and, should the number of applications exceed 15,000, 'an additional number of temporary residence permits may be granted, which will be governed by the annual maximum of the 4,000 temporary residence permits'. It is not known how the figure of 4,000 annual permits was calculated; arguably, it might prove necessary to grant them to a larger number of irregular Bangladeshis.

*142.* The criteria and the requirements for Bangladeshi nationals to be granted these temporary residence permits are laid down in Article 5 (for those living irregularly in Greece) and in Article 6 of the MoU (for those migrant workers who will come to Greece through regular (legal) migratory flows). For the first category, Article 5(1) provides that the following documents will be necessary: (a) a valid travel document, whose validity must cover at least two years after the date the application for the temporary residence permit has been submitted; (b) a valid work contract with an employer established in the Greek Territory or an employer's certificate that the applicant will be employed by him or by his company; and (c) proof of payment of the fees and costs envisaged in the legislation for the handling of the application. According to Article 5(3), these requirements are without prejudice to

216. Generally, *see* K. Minamide, 'The Temporariness of Bangladeshi Migration in Greece' 18(1) *Migration Letters* (2021) 61–71.

217. This provision should be read together with Art. 6(4) of the MoU, which says that the Greek authorities may notify on an annual basis the competent authorities of Bangladesh 'on the possible inclusion' of sectors, other than agriculture, based on Greece's labour needs. What is, however, not explained is the following: if, for example, tourism is another sector where Greece wishes to offer temporary employment to Bangladeshis for a period of five years, if after two years Greece decides to withdraw tourism from the eligible sectors, what will happen to those nationals of Bangladesh whose residence permits are still valid for one or more years?.

the general provisions of the Greek legislation pertaining to the acceptance of such applications. This provision should be read together with Article 7(2): The Hellenic Republic reserves the right to reject an application or withdraw a temporary residence permit if the applicant is considered to pose a threat to public security, public order, or public health. In such an eventuality, the consular authorities of Bangladesh shall be informed thereof, and they must provide full cooperation for the return of their nationals in question to Bangladesh.

*143.* The requirement that applicants must produce valid work contracts raised this rather important matter: considering that Article 23(1) of Law 5038/2023 (it will be analysed *infra*) provides that it is not permitted for employers to recruit and employ third-country nationals, who do not fulfil the conditions of legal residence in Greece, which employer will risk self-incrimination by supplying the contract of employment that is necessary for the application?

*144.* Furthermore, it is very interesting that Article 6(1) of the MoU provides that the documents to be produced in support of the application to be granted a temporary residence permit for seasonal employment include a valid work contract, which must specify the following: (a) the place and type of work; (b) the duration of the employment, which should be at least of one year; (c) the remuneration and the working hours; (d) the amount of any paid leave and other relevant working conditions; and (e) the date of commencement of employment. The difference in the content of Article 5(1) and Article 6(1) is striking: the former only requires some form of a contract or just an employer's confirmation of the existence of such a contract, while the latter demands the existence of an ordinary contract. Two further observations should be made. First, the MoU does not stipulate that the contract must be concluded in a language that the migrant worker understands. Second, there is no mention that the respective contracts must be concluded with employers whose businesses/companies are engaged in the agricultural sector (or any other seasonal sector that has been notified under the MoU). It follows that if the employer is engaged, for example, in the recycling industry, the employer cannot sign contracts for employment in agriculture.

## Chapter 3. Students and Researchers

*145.* The regulation of migration for educational reasons, another area governed by EU law under Directive 2016/801,[218] is laid down in Part VI of Law 5038/2023 (Articles 101–133). According to Article 101, the provisions of Part VI apply to third-country nationals who enter Greece for any of the following purposes: research, studies, internships or voluntary service. The following categories of third-country nationals are, *inter alia*, excluded from the application of Part VI: those residing in Greece as applicants of international protection or are entitled to international protection; those who have acquired the status of long-term residents in another EU Member State; those who have entered the territory of the EU as trainees in the context of intra-company transfers (Articles 53–58 of Law 5038/2023); those who have been accepted as highly skilled migrant workers (Articles 28–52 of Law 5038/2023). Moreover, the provisions of Part VI are subject to any more favourable conditions that derive from bilateral agreements or multilateral treaties, which have been concluded between the EU and third states, or from bilateral agreements or multilateral treaties concluded between the Hellenic Republic or more EU Member States and one or more third states. Finally, pursuant to Article 101(4), the competent Greek authorities are entitled to adopt or maintain more favourable provisions for certain categories of persons to whom Part VI applies.

### §1. Researchers

*146.* As regards entering the Greek territory for research purposes, the rationale of the Immigration Code is that foreign nationals will carry out research in the context of a specific research organization/centre/institution/body. The Greek State wants to control which these research organizations will be and, therefore, Article 103 of Law 5038/2023, which is titled 'Approval of research organisations', contains very detailed and elaborate provisions. In particular, Article 103(1) provides that any research organization, which is to receive a researcher in accordance with the entry and residence procedure defined in Part VI, must have been previously approved for this purpose. The approval is granted for a period of five years by the General Secretariat of Research and Innovation of the Ministry of Development, which will rely on their statutory mission and the proof that they conduct research. However, this procedure applies in practice only for private research organizations, because those that are governed by public law or those which are supervised by a public authority (e.g., the General Secretariat of Research and Innovation)[219] as well as (public) Universities are all considered to be approved bodies for the purposes of the Immigration Code. As far as private research organizations are concerned, the

218. Directive 2016/801 of the European Parliament and of the Council of 11 May 2016 on the conditions of entry and residence of third-country nationals for the purposes of research, studies, training, voluntary service, pupil exchange schemes or educational projects and au pairing, O.J. L 132, 21.5.2016, p. 21.

219. *See* a list at: https://gsri.gov.gr/en/supervised-bodies/.

conditions for being approved are laid down in Article 103(4); one of the conditions is to show that there is a necessity to employ third-country national researchers.

*147.* For a foreign researcher to reside in Greece, a contract must have been signed between him and the relevant research organization. Pursuant to Article 104, the researcher shall undertake the commitment to complete the research programme, and the organization shall undertake the obligation to host him for this very purpose. More specially, the hosting contract must contain the following information and clauses: (a) the purpose of the research activity; (b) the commitment by the third-country national that he will complete the research activity; (c) the research organization's undertaking that it will welcome the third-country national so as to complete the research activity; (d) the start and end dates or the estimated duration of the research activity; and (e) information about the researcher's intention of mobility to other EU Member States. However, under Article 104(3), before a research organization may sign a hosting contract, the research activity has been accepted by the competent bodies of the organization, while the purpose and estimated duration of the research activity, the availability of the essential financial resources to conduct the research as well as the qualifications of the third-country national have been confirmed. Finally, hosting contracts shall be automatically terminated in the following cases: the third-country national was not accepted as a researcher, the legal relationship between the researcher and the research organization ended, the researcher was not granted a residence permit or the research organization's approval by the General Secretariat of Research and Innovation was revoked.

*148.* As it transpires from the above provisions, the hosting agreement must have been signed before the researcher applies for a residence permit. Thus, Article 110 of Law 5038/2023 sets out the following six general requirements and conditions for being granted a research resident permit (type 'H.3'):

a. to hold a passport that is recognized by the Hellenic Republic, the validity of which will cover at least the duration of the intended stay for research, and to have obtained a national visa entry for the purpose of research;
b. to possess full health insurance cover, which will be valid for the duration of the intended stay;
c. to have sufficient financial resources to cover living expenses during the stay, without having to resort to the Greek social welfare system. The value of these resources (e.g., a grant, a scholarship, a valid employment contract, etc.) cannot be less than EUR 900 per month. All researchers must also be able to cover the expenses for the return trip. The evaluation of the adequate resources is based on individual examination of each application;
d. they do not pose a risk to public order, public safety and public health;
e. they have paid the fee of EUR 150 for being issued with the residence permit; and
f. they have submitted the hosting contract envisaged in Article 104.

*149.* The term of validity of a residence permit for research (type 'H.3') is equal to the duration of the hosting contract. If the latter is extended, upon the researcher's application, the permit may be extended for an equal period of time. According to Article 112 of Law 5038/2023, third-country nationals, who are categorized as 'researchers', are allowed to be accompanied by members of their family (they may also be joined by them at a later stage). The members of the researcher's family will be issued with a residence permit for family reunification within ninety days from the day a complete application has been submitted. Importantly, family members have unrestricted access to the job market and may also be self-employed. Finally, as regards the provisions on rejection, revocation or refusal to renew a research residence permit, these are laid down in Article 113(2). More specifically, this will happen, *inter alia*, in the following three cases:

a. the host organization has been declared bankrupt or has been placed under liquidation according to Greek insolvency law or it does not carry out any real economic activity or it has not fulfilled its obligations regarding social security, taxation, labour rights and working conditions or it has been sanctioned, according to the Greek legislation, for illegal employment;
b. there is adequate proof that the researcher resides in Greece for purposes other than those for which he was allowed to stay, i.e., his status as researcher is deemed to be a pretext for carrying out other activities; and
c. the host institution was established for the sole purpose of facilitating the entry of third-country nationals as researchers.

## §2. Students

*150.* Initially, it should be mentioned that the Immigration Code stipulates the issuance of residence permits for studies and for voluntary service. Overall, the same conditions and requirements are applicable to both these categories. Even though the present monograph deals only with permits for studies, the reader can assume that the same or similar provisions and procedures apply to the permits for voluntary service (some specific references will be made). Article 105 of Law 5038/2023 sets out the general conditions for the right of residence for the purpose of studies. These conditions, which must be cumulatively met, are the same as those mentioned above under Article 110 of Law 5038/2023 with the addition of a clause on third-country nationals who are under 18 years of age; they must provide the consent of parents or guardians for the duration of the intended stay as students. As regards the specific conditions that prospective students should meet, Article 106 mentions the following:

a. to have been admitted to a higher education institution in the Greek territory in order to attend a programme of studies;

b. to possess sufficient resources to cover the living expenses during the stay as well as to cover the return trip expenses.[220] As with the cases of foreign researchers, the Greek State does not want foreign students to become a burden to the national welfare system;
c. should the study programme to be followed require knowledge of the Greek language at a level of proficiency as a condition for the registration, a language diploma or certificate must be submitted together with the application; and
d. the tuition fees have been paid at the higher education institution.[221]

*151.* If the general and specific conditions are met and all necessary documents have been submitted, a residence permit for studies (type 'H.1') should be issued within a period of sixty days from the day the application was completed. Pursuant to Article 107(1) of Law 5038/2023, the residence permit for studies has a validity period of one year and may be renewed for an equal period, if the aforementioned conditions continue to be met.[222] However, the prospective student may apply from the beginning for a residence permit whose validity is equal to the maximum duration of the study programme that he intends to study. The total period of renewal of the residence permit may not exceed the total period of regular study, as laid down in the legislation. The same applies to postgraduate students and doctoral students. It should be noted that undergraduate University-level studies in Greece last for four years (the exception is study programmes at the so-called Polytechnics (engineers, civil engineers, architects, etc.) which is five years, and Medical Schools (six years)). The duration of postgraduate studies varies between twelve and twenty-four months. Doctoral studies ordinarily last for three years. Under Article 118, foreign students are allowed to work only part-time, outside study hours. The number of hours of work cannot be less than fifteen hours per week (or the equivalent in months per year).

*152.* Those holding a residence permit for studies with a validity period equal to the maximum duration of the study programme are required to submit to the relevant public authority, every two years, a certificate of registration and participation at the examinations as well as a certificate showing the grades attained. In case the holder has been registered for a postgraduate degree or for a doctorate, he must submit a detailed progress report. Pursuant to Article 107(3), if the holder does not comply with these obligations, the residence permit shall be revoked within two months from the expiration of the two-year period and the holder must leave the

220. *See* Joint Ministerial Decision 225679/2024, Determination of the amount and ways of proving the availability of sufficient resources provided for in the provisions of Law 5038/2023 and in other regulations, as well as the amount and ways of proving the required income for the application of the provisions of Arts 84 and 144 of Law 5038/2023, FEK 2024, Issue B' No. 5223.

221. Note that in the case of third-country nationals involved in voluntary service programmes, Art. 108 provides that they must have entered into an agreement with a host institution that is located in Greece. Should the host be a private organization, a certificate of compliance must be submitted showing that the programme has been approved or supervised by a public authority. There is no indication in the Immigration Code which this public authority might be.

222. Residence permits for voluntary service (type 'H.2') have also a validity period of one year and only in exceptional cases for a period of time equal to the duration of the voluntary programme.

Greek territory at once without the State being obliged to notify him an order to that effect. It follows that the foreign student may not argue that he was not aware that the residence permit had been revoked or cancelled.

*153.* Residence permits for studies and for voluntary services can be recalled and revoked for the reasons laid down in Article 113(1). These reasons include that the student does not show a satisfactory progress in his studies (the opinion of the relevant higher education institution must be sought) or that there is adequate proof that the student has been residing in Greece for purposes other than pursuing studies.

*154.* A common provision for holders of research and study permits and permits for work is Article 119, which regulates the stay of students and researchers for the purpose of looking for work or entrepreneurship. Thus, after completing their studies or the research project, holders of permits type 'H.1' and holders of permits type 'H.3' are allowed to remain in Greece, on the basis of the residence permit provided for in paragraph 3 of Article 119 and for a period of one year to search for employment or to set up a business that correspond to the level of the completed research or studies. To be issued with this special permit, the interested third-country national should apply at least thirty days before the expiration of the relevant permit. Article 119(8) provides that, after at least three months from the issuance of the special residence permit, holders are required to prove to the competent public authority that they have a real possibility to be hired or to set up a business. The Immigration Code does not however explain how the public authority is going to evaluate the evidence to be produced by holders.

*155.* Article 127 of Law 5038/2023 regulates the immigration status of children, who were born in Greece to parents holders of a residence permit for studies. To these children, in derogation of the applicable provisions of the legislation on family reunification of third-country nationals, an individual residence permit will be granted as members of the student's family. The permit will expire at the same time as the parents' residence permit and presumably, if the validity of the parents' permit is extended so will the child's permit. It is rather interesting that the Immigration Code does not have a similar provision for the holders of research residence permits. Article 127 also provides that a residence permit shall not be granted for study purposes to third-country nationals who reside in Greece for purposes of employment or for professional reasons, with the exception of those who have been admitted on the grounds of family reunification.

## Chapter 4. International Protection (Asylum)

*156.* As already mentioned, Greece has ratified the 1951 Refugee Convention and its 1967 Protocol. According to the definition of refugees given in Article 1 of the Convention, they are individuals who, owing to a well-founded fear of being persecuted for reasons of race, religion, nationality, membership of a particular social group or political opinion, have found themselves outside their country of nationality and are unable or, owing to such fear, unwilling to benefit from the protection of that country.

*157.* The position of Greek law is that every third-country national or stateless person,[223] who is at an official entry point or (already) on the Greek territory, has the right to apply for international protection (access to the asylum procedure is open and free of charge). However, there is a very important caveat: the persons applying must have not originated from a country which Greece designated as a safe country. It is irrelevant whether the persons in question have the nationality of the country in question (safe country of origin) or whether they were living in that country but had the nationality of another state (safe third country). What is taken into account to assess the safe country requirement is which had been the (last) country from which the applicant originated. In Greece, a modern Asylum Service was established in 2011.[224]

*158.* For Greece, the question of which are the safe countries is regulated in EU law, and, more specifically, in the so-called Asylum Procedures Directive.[225] According to it, a safe country of origin is considered to be a country where the law is applied in a (Western) democratic fashion, while the prevailing political circumstances do not consistently lead to persecution, torture, inhuman or degrading treatment or punishment, or threat by reason of indiscriminate violence in situations of international or internal armed conflict. The assessment of a 'safe country of origin' should take into account, *inter alia*, the following considerations/situations: the applicable laws and regulations of the country in question and how they are applied; the observance of human rights and fundamental freedoms, especially those from which no derogation is allowed (e.g., the right to life, the prohibition of slavery, the

223. Note that stateless persons are distinguished from refugees and are protected pursuant to the Convention relating to the Status of Stateless Persons, adopted on 28 Sep. 1954, entered into force on 6 Jun. 1960, 360 *UNTS* 117, ratified under Law 139/1975, FEK 1975 Issue A' No. 176, and the Convention on the Reduction of Statelessness, adopted on 30 Aug. 1961, entered into force on 13 Dec. 1975, 989 *UNTS* 175; Greece is not party to it.

224. *See* Law 3907/2011 on the establishment of an Asylum Service, *supra*.

225. Directive 2013/32/EU of the European Parliament and of the Council of 26 Jun. 2013 on common procedures for granting and withdrawing international protection, O.L. L 180, 29.6.2013, p. 60. *See also* the so-called Qualification Directive, Directive 2011/95/EU of the European Parliament and of the Council of 13 Dec. 2011 on standards for the qualification of third-country nationals or stateless persons as beneficiaries of international protection, for a uniform status for refugees or for persons eligible for subsidiary protection, and for the content of the protection granted (recast), O.J. L 337, 20.12.2011, p. 9. Both Directives were transposed under Law 4636/2019 on International Protection and other provisions, FEK 2019 Issue A' No. 169.

prohibition of torture and degrading treatment, etc.); respect for the non-refoulement principle; and the existence of a system of effective remedies against violations of the protected rights and freedoms. Should a third state be regarded as a safe country of origin, EU Member States usually include it in a national list. Once included, it will be presumed to be safe for applicants originating from that country unless evidence to the contrary can be adduced. In designating third states as safe, Member States are guided by the so-called Asylum Procedures Directive.[226]

*159.* As far as Greece is concerned, the criteria for accepting a third state as a safe country of origin were originally laid down in Article 86(1) of the aforementioned Law 4636/2019. The third paragraph of Article 86 provides that a joint decision of the Minister of Citizen Protection and the Minister of Foreign Affairs shall determine the third countries that are declared safe for certain categories of asylum seekers, according to their characteristics (racial, religious, etc.), and for the purposes of examining applications for international protection. An applicant for international protection may contest the application of the safe third country designation on the grounds that the third country of origin is not safe in his personal circumstances. The elements which will be taken into account for the issuance of this Joint Ministerial Decision include the domestic legislative regime of the third country in question as well as any bilateral or multilateral agreements that it has concluded (including with the EU).

*160.* These elements must always be up-to-date and come from authoritative sources of information, for example, from the official diplomatic sources of the country concerned, from the EU Agency for Asylum (EUAA),[227] the legislation of other EU Member States implementing the concept of safe third country of origin, from the Council of Europe, and/or from the United Nations High Commissioner for Refugees. The determination must be reviewed in November of each year. If there is a significant change in the human rights situation in a country designated as a safe third country, it shall be reviewed as soon as possible. Finally, the European Commission will be informed of all decisions on such designations.

*161.* However, three years later, Law 4636/2019 was abrogated, and a new legislative regime was adopted: Law 4939/2022, which is the current Code on International Protection.[228] The provision relevant to safe third countries is Article 91 of Law 4939/2022, whose third paragraph is a *verbatim* repetition of Article 86 of Law

---

226. Directive 2013/32/EU of the European Parliament and of the Council of 26 Jun. 2013 on common procedures for granting and withdrawing international protection (recast), O.J. L 180, 29.6.2013, p. 60.
227. EUAA is an agency of the European Union mandated with supporting Member States in applying the EU legislation on asylum, on international protection and on reception, also known as the Common European Asylum System (CEAS). It is located in Malta and its legal basis is Regulation 2021/2303 of the European Parliament and of the Council of 15 Dec. 2021 on the European Union Agency for Asylum and repealing Regulation (EU) No. 439/2010, O.J. L 468, 30.12.2021, p. 1. EUAA does not replace the Member States' national authorities on asylum and on international protection.
228. Law 4939/2022, Ratification of a Code of Legislation on reception, international protection of third-country nationals and stateless persons, and temporary protection in case of mass influx of

4636/2019. The presently valid ministerial decision was published on 15 December 2023 and lists the following countries as being safe: (a) Turkey as regards applicants for international protection, who originated from Syria or whose country of origin is Afghanistan, Pakistan, Bangladesh and Somalia; (b) Albania as regards applicants for international protection, who have irregularly entered the Greek territory through its borders with Albania; and (c) North Macedonia for applicants for international protection, who have irregularly entered the Greek territory from its border with North Macedonia.[229]

*162.* These determinations are, among others, based on the agreements on readmission, which have been concluded between the EU and these three third states.[230] Finally, it should be noted that the term 'safe third country' is regulated by EU law and, therefore, it is subject to the authentic interpretation by the CJEU. Thus, when asked by the Greek Council of State, the CJEU ruled that Member States may not issue a decision rejecting an asylum application as inadmissible on the basis of the concept of 'safe third country' when they have established that the asylum seeker will not be allowed to enter the territory of a country that is designated as safe. And it went on to say that a country may be listed as a 'safe third country' even if, despite its legal obligations, that third country has, in general and without any prospect of a contrary development, suspended the admission or readmission of those applicants to its own territory.[231]

## §1. Refugee Status

### I. Conditions, Procedures, Duration and Loss

*163.* In accordance with Article 69(1) of 4939/2022, third-country nationals or stateless persons have the right to submit an application for international protection. The application must be submitted before the so-called Receiving Authority, which must immediately complete the registration process, namely to record the applicant's identity details, his/her country of origin, perform a biometric identification, register a full statement of the reasons why the applicant requests international protection, as well as to record the place and address of residence and the language in

---

displaced aliens, FEK 2022 Issue A' No. 111. Note that several of its provisions have since been revised under the aforementioned Law 5078/2023 and Law 5130/2024.

229. Joint Ministerial Decision 538595/2023, Determination of third countries which are deemed to be safe and producing the national catalogue in accordance with Art. 91 of 4939/2022, FEK 2023 Issue B' No. 7063. It abrogated the previous Joint Ministerial Decision 734214/6.12.2022, FEK 2022 Issue B' No. 6250.

230. In particular, these are the Agreement between the European Community and the Republic of Albania on the readmission of persons residing without authorization, O.J. L 124, 17.5.2005, p. 22; the Agreement between the European Community and the former Yugoslav Republic of Macedonia on the readmission of persons residing without authorization, O.J. L 334, 19.12.2007, p. 7; and the Agreement between the European Union and the Republic of Turkey on the readmission of persons residing without authorization, O.J. L 134, 7.5.2014, p. 3.

231. CJEU, Case C-134/23, *Elliniko Symvoulio gia tous Prosfyges and Ypostirixi Prosfygon sto Aigaio*, Judgment, 4 Oct. 2024, ECLI:EU:C:2024:838.

which the application should be processed. However, if for any reason completing the registration is not possible, the Receiving Authority may proceed (at the latest within three working days from the submission of the application) to a partial recording of the minimum necessary information, which must include the language in which the application will be examined. In such a case, full registration must take place within the next fifteen working days. Article 69(7) of Law 4939/2022 envisages two other possibilities for applying for international protection. The first concerns third-country nationals or stateless persons when they are in a regime of restriction of liberty within a Reception and Identification Centre or a Closed Controlled Facility. The second concerns third-country nationals or stateless persons, who are detained in accordance with the applicable domestic legislation and who declare that they wish to lodge an application for international protection. In both cases, full registration (Article 69(1)) must take place as soon as possible.

*164.* Under Article 69(10) of Law 4939/2022, the applicant for international protection is also allowed to submit an application on behalf of his family members. However, should the latter be over 18 years of age and have full legal capacity, they must consent in writing to the submission of the application on their behalf. And before such consent is given, the adult family members in question must appear in person before the competent authorities and be informed about the relevant procedural consequences of submitting an application in person and about their right to submit an independent application for international protection. The existence of consent is required at the time of filing the application. As regards applicants who have entered the Greek territory with one or more children, they are allowed to lodge an application for international protection on behalf of the child/ren, supported by their birth certificates. If the application is filed after this applicant's application has been submitted, it shall be combined and processed at the stage the procedure for the applicant's application has reached.

*165.* Article 73(1) of Law 4939/2022 provides that applicants are allowed to remain in Greece until their application for international protection has been completed in the first instance. Their removal by any means is prohibited. However, the applicant's right to remain in Greece does not establish a right to be granted a residence permit. There are exceptions to this rule, which are laid down in the second paragraph of Article 73. More specifically, the applicant for international protection may: (a) be surrendered to another EU Member State on the basis of a European Arrest Warrant (EAW)[232] and in accordance with the provisions of Law 3251/2004;[233] (b) be extradited to a third state, with the exception of the applicant's country of origin (because otherwise the principle of non-refoulement would have been

232. The EAW is a simplified cross-border judicial surrender procedure for the purpose of prosecution or for executing a custodial sentence or detention order within the territory of EU Member States. The legal basis is Council Framework Decision of 13 Jun. 2002 (2002/584/JHA) on the European arrest warrant and the surrender procedures between Member States, O.J. L 190, 18.7.2002, p. 1. It has been in force since 1 Jan. 2004 in all EU Member States.

233. Law 3251/2004, European Arrest Warrant, amendment of Law 2928/2001 on criminal organizations and other provisions, FEK 2004 Issue A' No. 127, as lastly amended under Law 5108/2024,

violated); or (c) be extradited to an international criminal court, provided that the extradition will be legally justified on account of Greece's international obligations which must be observed. Currently, the only such international court would be the International Criminal Court, whose Statute[234] was ratified under Law 3003/2002.[235] The surrender or extradition must not lead to the direct or indirect refoulement of the person concerned, which would constitute a violation of Article 33(1) of the 1951 Convention or put the person concerned at risk of persecution or cause serious harm under the relevant provisions of Law 4939/2022, Article 7, Article 3 of the UN Convention against Torture,[236] Article 3 ECHR, Articles 4 and 19 of the EU Charter of Fundamental Rights and/or Article 5 of the Constitution, reference to which was made *supra*. In such cases, no applicant shall be surrendered or extradited before a final decision has been made on his application and for as long as fear of persecution exists in the requesting state.

*166.* Pursuant to Article 74 of Law 4939/2022, when submitting the application for international protection, applicants have the right to be informed in writing, in a language that they understand, and in a simple way, for example, which procedure will be followed; that they will have to appear in person at any stage of the procedure; what their rights are during their application being processed; that they have a duty to cooperate with the Greek authorities at each stage of the procedure; the consequences of breaching the duty to cooperate or not complying with their other obligations; etc. It should be noted that, under Article 79(2) of Law 4939/2022, all applications for international protection are initially considered for refugee status and, if the relevant conditions are not met, they will be considered for subsidiary protection status. Moreover, applicants must be informed of the consequences should their application be rejected, the possibilities of legally challenging it,[237] the deadline for filing an appeal against the decision rejecting the application, the authority before which it must be brought, and all other relevant information.[238] Applicants are ordinarily entitled to receive free legal assistance during this procedure,[239] and they always have the right to contact the UN High Commission for

---

Consolidation of the first instance of jurisdiction, spatial restructuring of civil and criminal justice courts and other provisions, FEK 2024 Issue A' No. 65.

234. Rome Statute of the International Criminal Court, adopted on 17 Jul. 1998, entered into force on 1 Jul. 2002, 2187 *UNTS* 3.

235. Law 3003/2002, Ratification of the Statute of the International Criminal Law, FEK 2002 Issue A' No. 75.

236. Convention against Torture and Other Cruel, Inhuman or Degrading Treatment or Punishment, adopted on 10 Dec. 1984, entered into force on 26 Jun. 1987, 1465 *UNTS* 85. Greece ratified it under Law 1782/1988, FEK 1988 Issue A' No. 116.

237. The legal remedies are those envisaged in the aforementioned Art. 24 of Law 2690/1999.

238. *See* further, Art. 8 of Law 4375/2016, Organization and operation of the Asylum Service, *infra*.

239. *See* further, Joint Ministerial Decision No. 788502/2023, Provision of legal aid to applicants for international protection, FEK 2023 Issue B' No. 42. The relevant 'Application for Legal Subscription' (as 'legal aid' has been translated in Greek) is available online in various languages, at: https://applications.migration.gov.gr/apps/type-7-applications/create.

Refugees (also known as 'UNHCR')[240] or any other certified organization that provides legal, medical and psychological assistance. Finally, applicants will be told about the possibility of their voluntary repatriation to their country of origin or country of nationality.

*167.* Pursuant to Article 74(5) and Article 75 of Law 4939/2022, applicants have the right to be granted an international protection applicant card once the registration and application process have been successfully concluded. This card is a temporary title essentially legitimizing the applicant's presence in Greece. While it does not establish a right to be issued with a residence permit, it ensures the enjoyment of the rights envisaged in the legislation and is necessary in order to conclude economic and other transactions. The card is valid for one year and is renewed until the examination process of the application for international protection has been completed, and the applicant is either recognized as a refugee or his application is rejected.

*168.* In case the application is rejected, the validity of the card automatically ends. However, the applicant may lodge an appeal against the rejection before the competent so-called Appeals Authority (the details are laid down in Articles 97 et seq. of Law 4939/2022).[241] Moreover, should the applicant fail to appear to renew the card before the last day of expiration, it shall automatically cease to be valid, save where the applicant can prove (documentary evidence is required) the existence of force majeure situations that had made the renewal impossible,

*169.* It is the general principle of the Code on International Protection that the decisions on the applications for international protection are taken on an individual basis, after a thorough, objective and impartial examination. To ensure it, the Asylum Service must search, collect, and evaluate accurate information about the political, social, economic, as well as the general situation prevailing in the countries of origin, which include the countries of previous habitual residence as well as the transit country or countries. For this purpose, on the one hand, it collects information from, among others, the EUAA, the UN High Commissioner for Refugees, and the relevant authorities in the other EU Member States, and, on the other hand, it ensures that the personnel examining and deciding on the applications is familiar with the national legislation, the relevant rules of international law as well as with the relevant jurisprudence on international protection (including the judgments of the ECtHR[242] and the conclusions of the so-called treaty bodies established under the UN human rights conventions, for example, the Human Rights Committee and the Committee against Torture).

240. For more information, *see* https://help.unhcr.org/greece/about-help-in-greece/contact-us/.
241. Note that the Appeals Authority is an administrative and not a judicial body.
242. For indicative purposes only, suffice to mention the following cases: ECtHR, Application No. 3566/16, *Alkhatib et autres c. Grèce*, Judgment, 16 Jan. 2024; Application No. 5418/15, *Safi and Others v. Greece*, Judgment, 7 Jul. 2022.

*170.* More specifically, Article 82, read in conjunction with Article 74 of Law 4939/2022, provides that, before a decision is reached, the Determining Authority must conduct a personal interview with the applicant (the details are laid down in Article 87),[243] which will take place with the assistance of an interpreter and, optionally, with the presence of one or more attorneys-at-law. During the interview, the Determining Authority must offer the applicant ample opportunity to present the information and documentation required to assess the application for international protection, including the statements that were made during the stage of registration. Interviews are audio recorded, signed and stored.

*171.* Furthermore, applicants are obliged to consent to a body search as well as to search of the objects that they carry, always in full compliance with the principles of human dignity and physical and psychological integrity. Applicants shall also be photographed, and, if they are over fourteen years of age, they will also be fingerprinted, in accordance with the domestic legislation. Article 85 of Law 4939/2022 provides that applicants may withdraw their application at any stage of the procedure, by submitting a relevant written statement and by handing in the international protection applicant card. This act of resignation must be certified in writing, always in the presence of an interpreter. Effectively, the applicant will find himself in the same position as if his application had been rejected at the last degree (i.e., his final appeal had not been successful). One major difference is that a (new) application for international protection may be submitted after the applicant has submitted the act of resignation (the new application shall be examined in accordance with the provisions of Article 94 of Law 4939/2022).

*172.* In accordance with Article 87(8) of Law 4939/2022, the decision to decline an application for international protection must state the factual and legal reasons that led to the rejection. Under Greek law, all administrative acts declining or rejecting an application must be fully reasoned.[244] This is a State obligation that derives principally from the rule of law, which is founded by Article 25(1) of the Constitution. What also derives from the rule of law is that the decision rejecting the provision of international protection may be appealed against before the competent organ/authority. But the allegedly affected third-country national must always bring the appeal within a specific period of time and also follow the prescribed procedure.

*173.* A decision granting international protection status to a foreigner may always be revoked. Pursuant to Article 96(1) of Law 4939/2022, when new information has emerged that constitutes a reason for reviewing the decision that granted it, the competent authority is compelled to examine whether there is a case for the withdrawal of this status. Based on what has just been said, this decision must set out the factual and legal reasons that justify the act of revocation and must give the

243. *See* further, Regulation No. 604/2013 of the European Parliament and of the Council of 26 Jun. 2013 establishing the criteria and mechanisms for determining the Member State responsible for examining an application for international protection lodged in one of the Member States by a third-country national or a stateless person (recast), O.J. L 180, 29.6.2013, p. 31.

244. *See* Art. 17 of the aforementioned Code of Administrative Procedure.

person in question adequate information on how to seek its reversal before the Appeals Authority. The judicial review of the decisions issued by the Appeals Authority may be requested by the applicant and also by the Minister of Immigration and Asylum. They shall be lodged with the competent administrative Court of First Instance, according to the provisions of the aforementioned Law 3068/2002. This is laid down in Article 114 of Law 4939/2022, which does not expressly stipulate whether the Minister of Immigration and Asylum may seek the judicial review of both the decision approving the status of international protection and the decision rejecting the application. Presumably, the Minister is empowered to do both, as he exercises supervision over all public authorities involved in asylum procedures.

*174.* Regarding access to employment for applicants for international protection, Article 192 of the aforementioned Law 5078/2023 amended the relevant provisions of Law 4939/2022, namely Article 57. Under the new rules, applicants for international protection have the right to access the labour market after sixty days from the completion of their application for international protection. More specifically, if they hold an 'applicant for international protection card' or an 'alien asylum seeker's card', which has been issued in accordance with the relevant legislation,[245] they are allowed to work as well as to provide their services throughout the validity period of the card. The right to access the labour market shall be automatically revoked in the event of a decision rejecting the application for international protection. It should be noted that said decision does not have a suspensory effect. Therefore, until an action for annulment has been lodged, the third county national in question has lost the right to remain in the country.

## II. Regulation of Temporary Protection

*175.* The sixth part of Law 4939/2022 (Articles 119 et seq.) contains separate provisions dealing with the temporary protection to be offered in instances of mass inflow of displaced aliens. Temporary protection in these circumstances is regulated under EU law (Directive 2001/55/EC).[246] According to Article 119, temporary protection does not prejudice the recognition of refugee status under the aforementioned Geneva Convention, while human rights and fundamental freedoms shall be

245. Namely: (a) Presidential Decree 113/2013, Establishment of a uniform procedure for granting refugee status or beneficiary of subsidiary protection to foreigners and stateless persons in compliance with Council Directive 2005/85/EC 'on minimum standards on procedures in Member States for granting and withdrawing refugee status' and other provisions, FEK 2013 Issue A' No. 146; (b) Art. 75 of Law 4939/2022; and (c) Presidential Decree 114/2010, Establishment of a uniform procedure for the recognition of refugee status or beneficiary of subsidiary protection for foreigners and stateless persons in compliance with Council Directive 2005/85/EC 'on minimum standards on procedures in Member States for granting and withdrawing refugee status', FEK 2010 Issue A' No. 195.

246. Council Directive 2001/55/EC of 20 Jul. 2001 on minimum standards for giving temporary protection in the event of a mass influx of displaced persons and on measures promoting a balance of efforts between Member States in receiving such persons and bearing the consequences thereof, O.J. L 212, 7.8.2001, p. 12.

respected and so shall the obligations regarding non-refoulement. The establishment, implementation and cessation of temporary protection will be regularly discussed with the UN High Commissioner for Refugees and other competent international organizations, which are not named in the legislation but presumably, include the EU (*see infra*) and the International Organization for Migration.

*176.* Article 120 of Law 4939/2022 sets the duration of temporary protection at one year and, if not terminated by a decision of the Council of the EU, it will be automatically extended for a period of six months. However, it may be extended for one more year if so determined by a Council decision under Article 4(2) of Directive 2001/55. It should be explained that any EU Member State can apply to the European Commission for the issuance of a Council decision on temporary protection, in accordance with Article 5(1) of Directive 2001/55. Thus, Article 121 of Law 4939/2022 stipulates that, with the care of the Ministry of Immigration and Asylum, an application for temporary protection can be submitted to the European Commission and will include a description of the special groups of people to whom temporary protection will be applied, the effective date of commencement of temporary protection and an estimation of the size of displaced persons' flows. Should a Council decision be issued, and before its expiration, the Ministry of Immigration and Asylum can submit a request to the European Commission for the termination of the temporary protection provided, if it considers that it is no longer warranted to deal with the situation for which it was established in the first place.

*177.* The instances where third-country nationals shall be excluded from temporary protection are laid down in Article 143 of Law 4939/2022. More specifically they refer to the following situations: (a) there is sufficient evidence that they have committed, either as direct perpetrators or as instigators, crimes against peace, war crimes or crimes against humanity as defined by international law[247] or have committed a serious, non-political, crime outside the territory of Greece at a time before they were admitted in Greece for temporary protection;[248] (b) they have been found guilty of acts contrary to the purposes and principles of the UN;[249] and (c) they have been convicted by an irrevocable court decision for a particularly serious crime, on the basis of which he is considered dangerous to national security and/or to public

247. It is not always clear how international law defines and understands these international crimes; however, the Elements of Crime, which have been adopted in the context of the International Criminal Court, may provide adequate definitions as well as elaborate on their content. The Elements of Crime are presently accepted by 124 states, online available at https://www.icc-cpi.int/sites/default/files/Publications/Elements-of-Crimes.pdf.

248. According to Art. 143(1), to exclude the applicant from protection, the nature of the crime for which he is suspected shall be taken into account. In the case of very serious crimes committed, they may be characterized as non-political, even if they were committed with an alleged political goal. The provision of Art. 143 applies not only to the perpetrators but also to the instigators of the crimes.

249. This provision is rather vague, considering that the UN purposes and principles (Arts 1–2 UN Charter) concern sovereign states and not individuals. Effectively, natural persons are ordinarily not able to act against these purposes and principles on their own, with the probable exception of heads of state, military commanders, etc., in cases where there was a use of violence or threat of the use of violence.

order (*ordre public*). These grounds of exclusion are always based solely on the personal conduct of the persons concerned, who will also benefit from the principle of proportionality when decisions or exclusion measures are taken.

*178.* Finally, Article 194 of the aforementioned Law 5078/2023 provides that third-country nationals, who are beneficiaries of temporary protection in accordance with Articles 120 et seq. of Law 4939/2022 and hold a valid residence permit, may, by way of derogation from Law 5038/2023, apply for a residence permit for one of the categories of residence permits laid down in the Immigration Code. Applicants must comply with all the relevant requirements envisaged for being issued with the residence permit they applied for, with the (obvious) exception of the possession of an entry visa.

## III. Subsidiary Protection

*179.* The question of subsidiary protection, a form of international protection, is regulated by EU law and, therefore, Greece has to apply the relevant EU rules. According to Article 2(g) of the aforementioned 'Qualification Directive', subsidiary protection status means the recognition by a Member State of a third-country national or a stateless person as a person eligible for subsidiary protection. And pursuant to Article 2(f), the persons eligible for subsidiary protection also those third-country nationals or stateless persons, who do not qualify as refugees but who show substantial grounds leading to the conclusion that, if they were returned to the country of origin (in the case of stateless persons, to the former habitual residence), they would face a real risk of suffering serious harm and owing to such risk, they are unwilling to avail themselves of that country's protection. It follows that the two crucial elements of subsidiary protection are real risk (a factual assessment) and serious harm (a more actual assessment). What constitutes 'serious harm' is defined in Article 15 of the 'Qualification Directive' as either of the following three situations: (a) the imposition of death penalty or execution; (b) torture or inhuman or degrading treatment or punishment of an applicant in the country of origin; or (c) serious and individual threat to a civilian's life or person by reason of indiscriminate violence in situations of international or internal armed conflict.

*180.* However, not all third-country nationals, who meet the above definition will be granted subsidiary protection status. And this is because Article 17 of the 'Qualification Directive' lays down several exceptions, which, on the whole, have to do with third-country nationals' (criminal) behaviour and acts. Thus, third-country nationals or stateless persons shall be excluded from seeking subsidiary protection status, if there are serious reasons to consider that they: (a) have committed crimes against peace, war crimes, or crimes against humanity 'as defined in the international instruments drawn up to make provision in respect of such crimes'; (b) have perpetrated a serious crime; (c) are guilty of acts contrary to the purposes and principles of the UN, as set out in the Preamble and Articles 1 and 2 of its Charter;[250] or (d) constitute a danger to the community or to the security of the Member State in which they are present. Article 17(2) stipulates that the exclusion does not only apply to the perpetrators of these crimes and acts but also to those persons, who incite or otherwise participate in their commission. It follows from the wording of Article 17 that it is up to each EU Member State to provide in their domestic legislation what are the 'serious crimes' and what a 'danger to the community or security' entails.

*181.* This being the general framework, in the Greek legal order subsidiary protection is presently regulated in the aforementioned Law 4939/2022, which was lastly amended by Law 5130/2024. As regards the recognition of third-country nationals as persons eligible for subsidiary protection, Article 14 of Law 4939/2022 repeats verbatim the provision of Article 15 of the 'Qualification Directive'. Regarding the exclusion from subsidiary protection status, Article 16(1) of Law 4939/2022 defines as 'serious crimes' the following (in brackets the relevant provision in the Penal Code): any felony or any misdemeanor, which is punishable by a sentence of imprisonment of at least three years as well as abduction of minors (Article 324 Penal Code); grievous bodily harm (Article 310 Penal Code); bodily harm to weak persons (Article 312 Penal Code); rape (Article 336 Penal Code); violation of sexual dignity (Article 337(2)–(4) Penal Code); sexual acts with or in front of minors (Article 339 Penal Code); abuse of minors (Article 342 Penal Code); pornography of minors (Article 348A Penal Code); attraction of children for sexual reasons (Article 348B Penal Code); pimping (Article 349 Penal Code); sexual acts with a minor for remuneration (Article 351A Penal Code); robbery (Article 380 Penal Code); and extortion (Article 385 Penal Code). Moreover, what constitutes a danger to Greece's national security or society means that the third-country national has been convicted by a final Court judgment for committing a serious crime as defined in Article 16(1). Moreover, the provision of Article 16(3) adds another head of exclusion. More specifically, there shall be no entitlement to subsidiary protection if, before entering the country, the third-country national has committed one or more crimes, other than those referred to Article 16(1), which would have resulted in a custodial sentence had they been committed in Greece, and he or she left his/her country of origin solely to avoid sanctions as a result of those crimes, unless the penalties in the country of origin are disproportionate to the penalty provided for the same crime in Greece.

*182.* Article 15 of Law 4939/2022 regulates the cessation of subsidiary protection. In particular, third-country nationals or stateless persons shall no longer be entitled to this status, if the circumstances which led to its recognition have ceased to exist or have changed to such an extent that the protection granted is no longer necessary. However, any beneficiary of subsidiary protection, who is able to invoke

250. These two provisions set out, respectively, the goals and the principles of the United Nations. Of course the duties and obligations set out therein concern the UN Member States and not individuals.

compelling reasons arising from previous serious harm in order to refuse the protection afforded to him/her by the country of nationality (in the case of statelessness, the country of his/her previous habitual residence) may continue holding this status.

*183.* Cessation of subsidiary protection is linked to but is regulated separately from revocation or refusal to renew this status, the latter being regulated in Article 18 of Law 4939/2022. Thus, if entitlement to subsidiary protection in accordance with Article 15 has ceased, the status shall be revoked, or not renewed. Furthermore, it shall be revoked or refused to be renewed if the third-country national in question (the beneficiary) ought to have been excluded from the right to subsidiary protection, in accordance with the aforementioned Article 16(3). Finally, the beneficiary will have the status revoked or not renewed if he was awarded obtained subsidiary protection by using false documents or by distorting crucial facts or if the provisions of Article 16(1) and (2) apply to him/her. As is expressly stated in Article 18(4), the applicant for subsidiary protection status is obliged to disclose any relevant information and submit any pertinent document at his/her disposal.

*184.* In short, the Greek authorities will grant subsidiary protection status to any person, who does not meet the criteria for being given the refugee status, but there are substantial grounds to believe that he/she runs a serious risk of suffering serious harm in his/her country of origin or habitual residence. The reasons might be that the applicant would be in danger of facing the death penalty or execution, or be subjected to torture or inhuman or degrading treatment, or because his/her life or physical integrity would be threatened as a result of an ongoing international conflict or a domestic armed conflict in the country of origin.

*185.* In practice, all third-country nationals within the Greek territory have the right to apply for international protection. They will undergo a personal interview with a case worker of the Asylum Service. At some stage, the Asylum Service will issue a decision, which will have one of the following three outcomes: grant refugee status or grant subsidiary protection status or reject the application. What will determine the outcome are the statements made during the personal interview, the information provided substantiating the application, information regarding the country of origin and any other information contained in the applicant's file. When the Asylum Service has set the date for the interview, applicants will receive an 'International Protection Applicant Card', which is valid for not more than one year. In the meantime, applicants will have been issued with a Tax Identification Number (TIN) and a provisional Insurance and Health Care Number, which will enable them to be employed. The decision granting subsidiary protection status is not final, in the sense that the beneficiary, who considers that he/she were entitled to refugee status, has the right to appeal before the Appeals Authority within the deadline specified in the decision. Even if the appeal is rejected, the beneficiary will not lose the status. Therefore, there seems to be no good reason why he/she should not lodge an appeal. Even if the beneficiary is not successfully in being granted the refugee status, he/she will not lose the subsidiary protection status.

## Chapter 5. Humanitarian Statutes

*186.* Part G of the Immigration Code regulates residency for humanitarian and other special reasons. It comprises only one provision, namely Article 134 of Law 5038/2023. Under the first paragraph of Article 134, the Minister of Immigration and Asylum has the power and the discretion to grant a residence permit on a case-by-case basis for humanitarian reasons to third-country nationals who are already living in Greece (residence permit type 'A.1' – Ad Hoc Residence Permit). These permits, the holders of which have the right to access the labour market, are granted to victims as well as to important witnesses of criminal acts; victims of domestic violence; victims of crimes having racist characteristics; to those suffering from serious health problems (provided that they are holders of a valid (not expired) residence permit); to victims of work accidents; to those who follow a State approved mental health treatment programme; and to third-country nationals who, at the risk of their lives, carried out acts of social virtue and acts of solidarity that promote the values of humanism.

*187.* Moreover, under the second paragraph of Article 134, the Minister of Immigration and Asylum has the right to grant residence permits for humanitarian grounds with the right to access the labour market to third-country nationals who are present in Greece and fall into one of the following two categories:

a. Residence permits type 'A.2': victims of human trafficking who fall into the ambit of the so-called Palermo Protocol[251] and do not come under the provisions of Articles 135 to 142 of Law 5038/2023; or
b. Residence permits type 'A.3': third-country nationals, who were employed either with particularly abusive working conditions or while being minors, according to Article 89 of the aforementioned Law 4052/2012 (it transposed EU Directive 2009/52 on sanctions against employers of illegally staying third-country nationals).

*188.* These residence permits are valid for one year and may be renewed for an equal period, as long as the grounds for which they were issued continue to exist. Should they no longer exist, the holder may request a change in the category of residence permit according to Article 12 of Law 5038/2023, which, however, does not stipulate if they are allowed to apply for all other types of residence permits or only for certain ones.

251. Protocol to United Nations Convention against Transnational Organized Crime to Prevent, Suppress and Punish Trafficking in Persons, especially Women and Children, adopted by UN General Assembly Resolution 55/25, 'United Nations Convention against Transnational Organized Crime', 15 Nov. 2000, entered into force on 25 Dec. 2003, 2237 *U.N.T.S* 319. Greece ratified it under Law 3875/2010, Ratification and application of the United Nations Convention against Transnational Organized Crime and of the three Protocols to it and relevant provisions, FEK 2010 A' No. 158.

*189.* Furthermore, pursuant to Article 134(4), the Secretary of the competent Decentralized Administration is empowered to grant residence permits for humanitarian reasons to third-country nationals who live in Greece and fall into one of the following categories:

a. Residence permits type 'A.4', which may be issued to *(aa)* adult aliens, who are unable to attend to their affairs due to health reasons, or minors, who are demonstrably in need of protection and are hosted by institutions or other public benefit organizations, provided that their return to a safe environment is not possible; *(ab)* minors, whose custody has been assigned by a decision of a Greek court of justice or by a foreign court of justice, which is recognized by the Greek authorities, to Greek families or to families of third-country nationals having their legal residence in Greece, or minors for whom adoption proceedings are pending before the Greek authorities; or *(ac)* minor third-country nationals, who have been placed in a foster family either by means of a decision of a Greek court of justice or by the legal guardians;
b. Residence permits type 'A.5' to be issued to minors, who live in boarding schools operating under the supervision of the competent Ministries.

*190.* The residence permits of type 'A.4' and of type 'A.5' are valid for three years and are renewed for an equal period of time if the conditions and circumstances on the basis of which they were issued are still present. As above, if they are discontinued, a change of category of residence permit may be possible (Article 12 of Law 5038/2023). Presumably, since this category of permits relates to minors, the legislator should have considered that the conditions might have changed but the holder, being as it were a minor, might not be in a position to act before the competent immigration authorities. Notwithstanding this submission, Article 134(8) provides that applications for being granted residence permits for minors (also for adults), who are unable to take care of their own affairs and are hosted in institutions, can validly be submitted by the legal representative of the institution in question.

*191.* Finally, in accordance with Article 134(4), the Secretary of the competent Decentralized Administration is empowered to grant residence permits for exceptional reasons with the right to access the labour market to third-country nationals who have either lived in Greece for at least seven continuous years prior to the submission of the application[252] or who are parents of a Greek national. An examination fee of EUR 300 must be paid for the application for this type of residence permit (type 'A.6') to be considered.

252. The requirement of seven year presence in Greece existed under the Immigration and Social Integration Code as well; *see* further, Decision of the Minister of Migration Policy No. 18951/22.6.2018 on the determination of the documents of certain date proving the seven years of continuous residence in the country of a third-country national who applies for a residence permit for exceptional reasons, FEK 2018 Issue B' No. 2487.

§1. VICTIMS OF SMUGGLING AND/OR THB

*192.* The relevant section of the Immigration Code is Part H (Articles 135 et seq. of Law 5038/2023), which is titled 'Admission of Third Country Citizens – Victims of Trafficking in Human Beings or Illegal Trafficking of Immigrants According to Directive 2004/81/EC'.[253] As stated, this is another area that is regulated by EU law. However, as Greece is a contracting party to the Convention on Action against THB,[254] which has been concluded under the auspices of the Council of Europe, domestic legislation must comply with its provisions as well.

*193.* Article 135(1) of Law 5038/2023 regulates the so-called period of reflection granted to the victims of THB. More specifically, third-country nationals, who have been designated as THB victims or have been involved in migrant smuggling in the meaning of Article 4(k) and 4(l) of Law 5038/2024 and are not subject to Article 1(2) of Presidential Decree 233/2003,[255] will be granted by the competent office of the public prosecutor a reflection period of three months, in order to escape from the influence of the perpetrators of the crimes against them and to recover mentally so that they can make a consciously unaffected decision about their cooperation with the public prosecutor. In the case of victims who are minors, a further period of two months may be granted. Overall, minors, including unaccompanied minors, are entitled to special care under Article 136 of Law 5038/2024.

*194.* Article 4(k) of Law 5038/2024 gives the following definition of the term 'victim of trafficking of human beings': the natural person (individual) for whom there are reasonable grounds to be considered a victim of any of the crimes that are provided for in Article 323A, in Article 339(1) and (3), in Article 342(1) and (2), in Article 348(2), as well as in Articles 348a, 348b, 349 and 351A of the Penal Code, before criminal prosecution has been lodged against the alleged perpetrators as well as the natural person against whom any of the above crimes have been committed and for which criminal proceedings have been initiated.[256] It is of no consequence

253. Council Directive 2004/81/EC of 29 Apr. 2004 on the residence permit issued to third-country nationals who are victims of trafficking in human beings or who have been the subject of an action to facilitate illegal immigration, who cooperate with the competent authorities, O.J. L 261, 6.8.2004, p. 19.

254. CETS No. 197, signed on 16 May 2005, entered into force on 1 Feb. 2008, ratified under Law 4216/2013, FEK 2013 Issue A' No. 266. Note that the Greece signed the Council of Europe Convention against Trafficking in Human Organs, CETS No. 216, when it opened for signature on 25 Mar. 2015 (it entered into force on 1 Mar. 2018) but has not yet ratified it. *See* further, Agreement between the Government of the Hellenic Republic and the Council of Ministers of Albania for the protection and assistance of children victims of trafficking, signed in Tirana on 27 Feb. 2006, ratified under Act 3692/2008, FEK 2008 Issue A' No. 173.

255. Presidential Decree 233/2003, Protection and assistance according to Art. 12 of Law 3064/2002 (FEK 2002 Issue A' No. 248) to victims of crimes of Arts 323, 323A, 323B, 348A, 349, 351 and 351A of the Penal Code, and Arts 87(5) and (6) and 88 of Law 3386/2005, FEK 2003 Issue A' No. 204. Article 1(2) reads as follows: 'For the purposes [of this Presidential Decree] victims … are defined as those persons, nationals or foreigners, who have suffered direct damage to their physical integrity or to their personal or sexual freedom or there is a serious risk to their integrity, freedom or life.'

256. *See* Anagnostopoulos and Magliveras, *Criminal Law in Greece*, *supra* n. 66, pp. 115–117.

whether the individuals in question entered the Greek territory legally or illegally. The characterization 'victim of trafficking in human beings' is given by a decision of the competent Public Prosecutor of First Instance and will be issued regardless of whether the victim cooperates with the prosecuting authorities or not. In doing so, the legislator has taken into consideration the reality that THB victims face, namely that they very often are unwilling to cooperate with the authorities due to threats directed against members of their family who live in Greece or in the country of origin.

*195.* Article 4(l) of Law 5038/2023 gives the following definition of the term 'victim of migrant smuggling': the individual in respect of whom there are reasonable grounds to be considered a victim of any of the offences referred to Article 24(5) and (6) and in Article 25 of Law 5038/2023, when they were committed by a criminal organization before criminal proceedings are brought as regards these offences as well as the individual against whom, one of the above-mentioned offences was perpetrated and in respect of which criminal proceedings have been initiated, provided that in both cases the persons in question entered the Greek territory irregularly.

*196.* According to Article 135(3) of Law 5038/2023, during the period of reflection, the victims shall not be removed from Greece. Equally, decisions ordering a return to the country of origin, which have been issued but not yet executed, shall be suspended. However, in the following cases, the competent public prosecutor's office may decide to end the reflection period before its expiration:

a. the victim in question has actively, voluntarily and on his own initiative reunited with the perpetrators of the crimes laid down in the aforementioned Article 4(k) and 4(l) of Law 5038/2023;
b. the facts that had been taken into account to classify the third-country national as a THB victim were not true; and
c. there are compelling reasons for public order and public security.

*197.* During the reflection period, THB victims and migrant smuggling victims are entitled to the benefits envisaged in Article 137 of Law 5038/2023. In particular, they have the right to health care and access to psychological services, which are offered by the National Health System and other bodies and entities coopering with it,[257] as well as to the Reception and Identification Service.[258] Additionally, all

257. *See* further, Arts 2 to 4 of Presidential Decree 233/2003, *supra*.
258. It was established in 2016 under Law 4375/2016, Organization and operation of the Asylum Service, the Appeals Authority, the Reception and Identification Service, the establishment of a General Secretariat for Reception – Adaptation of Greek legislation to the provisions of Directive 2013/32/EU of the European Parliament and of the Council 'on common procedures for granting and withdrawing international protection (recast)' (L 180/29.6.2013) – Provisions on the employment of beneficiaries of international protection and other provisions, FEK 2016 Issue A' No. 51. Its primary mission is the reception and identification of third-country nationals or stateless persons, who have entered the Greek territory through unofficial routes.

victims will be guaranteed adequate subsistence if they do not have sufficient financial resources or other means of subsistence. Finally, the competent prosecuting, judicial and police authorities must, as a matter of priority, ensure that victims are provided with translation and interpretation services as required, that they are informed of their legal rights and that they receive all necessary legal aid.

*198.* Pursuant to Article 138 of Law 5038/2023, third-country nationals, who have been identified as THB victims or migrant smuggling victims, which practically means that a decision to that effect has been issued by the competent Public Prosecutor of First Instance (Article 135), shall be granted a specific residence permit for victims (residence permit type 'A.7') or shall have the existing permit renewed without the payment of a fee. The conditions and the procedure to be applied for granting these permits are set out in Articles 139 to 142 of Law 5038/2023.

*199.* In particular, as regards the conditions, Article 139 of Law 5038/2023 stipulates that, after the expiration of the reflection period, the competent Public Prosecutor examines whether one of the following circumstances are present and draws up a report: (a) it is deemed appropriate to extend the victim's stay in the Greek territory, in order to facilitate the ongoing investigation or criminal prosecution; (b) the victim has demonstrated a clear willingness to cooperate; and (c) the victim has severed all relations with the alleged perpetrators of the THB or smuggling offences (*infra*, Article 4(k) and 4(l) of Law 5038/2023). Subject to grounds of public order and public security, the residence permit will be issued for twelve months. Should one of the above three conditions continue to be met, the permit will be renewed each time for another period of twelve months. This type of permit, according to Article 140, ensures that the holder has the right to access the labour market, to be given the benefits and care laid down in Article 137 as well as access to vocational training and education.[259]

*200.* In certain cases, the residence permit can be revoked or the application for renewal can be denied. These instances are laid down in Article 141 of Law 5038/2023 and have mostly to do with the behaviour of the holder – THB victim:

a. he has reconnected actively and voluntarily with the suspected perpetrator/s of the criminal offence/s;
b. the competent authorities have good reasons to believe that his cooperation or his original complaint for THB or for migrant smuggling was fraudulent;
c. there are grounds of public policy and public security that justify the revocation or the refusal; and

259. *See* further, Arts 5 and 6 of Presidential Decree 233/2003, *supra*.

d. the criminal proceedings for the offences of Article 4(k) or 4(l) of Law 5038/2023 have been terminated, as provided for in Article 43 or Article 47 of the CCP.[260]

260. Article 43 CCP concerns those instances where a criminal prosecution is finally determined not to be brought against the alleged perpetrator or is for other reasons archived. Article 47 CCP is about the so-called public interest witnesses, namely those who assist the prosecution authorities with crucial information or revealing unknown events, etc., and, in exchange, they are not prosecuted.

# Part IV. Residence Rights of Family Members (Family Reunification)

*201.* Part D of the Immigration Code (Articles 83 et seq. of Law 5038/2023) regulates family reunification, which is another area of immigration subject to EU law, the principal legal instrument being Directive 2003/86.[261] According to Article 83(1), the relevant provisions shall apply where the third-country national, who wants to proceed with family reunification (the term 'sponsor' is used),[262] holds a residence permit, which has been issued by the competent Greek authorities for a duration of at least two years. A third-country national legally residing in Greece for a period of two years is entitled to request that his family members enter the country to live with him. Even though Article 84(1) provides that the application for what is effectively family reunification shall be submitted and examined when the family members reside outside the Greek territory, it goes on to say that, in case they were residing in Greece before the application was submitted, this will not be a reason preventing the application to be made.

*202.* There are certain conditions that the sponsor must meet to exercise the right to a family relationship. Over and above the obvious requirement to prove the family relationship with the persons for whom reunification is sought, the sponsor must fulfil, cumulatively, the following three basic conditions: (a) accommodation capable of meeting his own needs and those of the family members; (b) a personal income, which is stable, regular and adequate to cover his own needs and those of his family, without having to resort to Greece's social security system. As regards the amount of the income, it cannot be less than the annual net income based on the applicable minimum wage in Greece, increased by 20% for the spouse and 15% for each child;[263] and (c) a comprehensive health insurance cover, whose coverage is equal to what Greek nationals are covered for, and which can also extend to cover all family members. Pursuant to Article 84(3) of Law 5038/2023 in case of

261. Council Directive 2003/86/EC of 22 Sep. 2003 on the right to family reunification, O.J. L 251, 3.10.2003, p. 12.
262. *See* the definition in Art. 2(c) of Directive 2003/86: 'sponsor' means a third-country national residing lawfully in a Member State and applying or whose family members apply for family reunification to be joined with him/her.
263. The presently legal minimum (daily) wage and the minimum (monthly) salary are laid down in Ministerial Decision 25058/29/3/2024, FEK 2024 Issue B' 1974; they have been in force since 1 Apr. 2024.

polygamy, if the sponsor already has a spouse living with him in Greece, family reunification with another spouse is not possible.

*203.* Once the request for family reunification has been received, Article 85 of Law 5038/2023 stipulates that the competent public authority must immediately request the opinion of the relevant Police authority for matters relating to public policy and public security, as well as the opinion of the competent Greek consular authority to have the existence of the family relationship verified. The latter will be ascertained by means of personal interviews with the members of the family; the non-appearance of family members for an interview will make the request inadmissible. Consideration of risks arising for the protection of public health will also be taken into account. The opinion to be given by the Police and by the relevant consular authority must be provided within an exclusive period of three months following the request. The family reunification procedure must have been completed within nine months following the submission of the application. Once a residence permit has been granted to the members of the sponsor's family, Article 89 provides that they shall be on an equal footing with the sponsor as regards the right to education, training, and vocational guidance as well as access to work.

*204.* In accordance with Article 86 of Law 5038/2023, each family member entering the Greek territory for the purpose of reunification must apply to be issued a residence permit before the entry visa expires. All permits to be granted are individual permits and this applies to minor children as well. However, in accordance with Article 87, the initial permit that family members will be granted shall expire on the same day that the sponsor's residence permit expires. And when the application for renewal is made, the right of residence of family members will follow the fate of the sponsor's permit. There is an exception: in case the sponsor acquires the status of long-term resident, the residence permit of the members of his family will be (initially) granted for three years and then renewed every three years. During the examination of an application for renewal, the Immigration Code demands that the sponsor proves that he still maintains the family relationship with his dependent family members and that he has fulfilled all social security and tax obligations towards the Greek State. In practice, this means that the employee social security contributions have been paid in full and that the annual tax returns have been filed and any tax due has been paid to the Inland Revenue Service.

*205.* Article 88 of Law 5038/2023 sets out the grounds and instances where a residence permit for family reunification shall not be granted, shall be withdrawn or shall not be renewed:

a. the competent public authority regards that there exists a risk to public order and public security. In case the risk exists because the third-country national has committed an offence, the seriousness or the type of the offence committed shall be taken into account as well as the extent to which he poses a threat;
b. there exist public health reasons;
c. the sponsor and/or the members of his family ceased to lead a genuine marital or family life;

d. official documents or judgments rendered by a court of justice reveal that, during the application procedure, false or misleading information and/or falsified documents were used, that fraud was committed or that other illegal means were employed to secure the approval of the application; and
e. it has been established that the family relationship (e.g., marriage, adoption of family members or recognition of children) was created for the sole purpose of circumventing the conditions of family reunification and for obtaining entry into Greece or for being granted the right of residence.

*206.* However, Article 88 also stipulates that even if the above grounds exist before an application is rejected or a residence permit is revoked or its renewal is refused and before a removal order against the sponsor or members of his family is made, the competent authorities must take into account the stability of the sponsor's family, the duration of his stay in Greece as well as the existence of any family, cultural and social ties with their country of origin. To put it otherwise, the competent authorities must balance the established risk to public security, public order or public health with the ties that the sponsor and the members of his family have established with the Greek society and the lack of ties with the country of origin.

*207.* The requirements for a family member to be able to obtain an independent (autonomous) residence permit are laid down in Article 90 of Law 5038/2023 (residence permit Type 'O.2'): at least five years of residence in Greece and not be in possession of a residence permit other than a permit issued for reasons of family reunification. This type of permit concerns the spouse of the sponsor or the person with whom the sponsor lives together (cohabitation) and the child (or children) who has reached the age of majority. Moreover, an autonomous residence permit may be issued to family members, for whom the right to family reunification has been exercised if the sponsor has died (the family member must however have already lived in Greece for one year) or in the event of divorce, marriage annulment or proven separation.[264]

264. As these are family law matters, Art. 90 refers to the provisions of Art. 1441 of the Hellenic Civil Code on divorce by mutual consent, which will be applied by analogy. In a nutshell, Art. 1441 of the Civil Code provides that the spouses may, by written agreement (or by means of a joint digital statement), decide to dissolve their marriage. The written agreement is drawn up between the spouses in the presence of two attorneys, one for each of them. If there are under-aged children, in order for the marriage to be dissolved, the written agreement (or the joint digital statement) must also regulate in some detail the division of parental responsibility, i.e., who will have the custody of the children, where their place of residence will be, with whom parent will they live, what arrangements have been agreed to secure their contact with the other parent, who will pay for their expenses, for their schooling, etc. This agreement shall be valid for at least two years and shall be automatically extended, if neither parent express the willingness to have it terminated. These written agreements (or digital statements) are subsequently passed on to a notary public, who draws up a legal act (deed) by virtue of which the marriage is terminated. The actual dissolution will take effect at a later stage when a copy of the notarial deed has been deposited with the registry office where the marriage was registered. These registries should be understood as the public offices where all events that have to do with an individual are recorded (birth, name giving, baptizing, marriage, death, etc.). Traditionally, each municipality has its own registry. The duration of these

autonomous residence permits may not exceed three years but, at any time within the period of validity, the holder is allowed to file an application to change the category of the residence permit. If the application is successful, the presence of the third-country national in Greece will no longer depend on the sponsor and, presumably, there will no longer be any family reunification.

# Part V. Sanctions

*208.* In the Immigration Code, the question of sanctions (whether administrative, criminal or disciplinary) is addressed in the context of the various duties and obligations which must be fulfilled by different categories of persons. More specifically, the relevant provisions of Law 5038/2023 are structured as follows: (a) sanctions to be imposed on third-country nationals (Article 20); (b) sanctions to be imposed on employees of public authorities, which principally include legal persons governed by public law, local administration authorities, and social security organization (Article 21); (c) sanctions to be imposed on employers of migrant workers (Article 23); (d) sanctions to be imposed on private individuals, including third-country nationals (Article 24); and (e) sanctions to be imposed on masters/captains of ships, vessels or aeroplanes as well as to drivers of all kinds of means of transporting third-country nationals from abroad to Greece (Article 25). They will now be examined in that order.

## §1. Sanctions Imposed on Third-Country Nationals

*209.* As has been mentioned, Article 19 of Law 5038/2023 sets out certain (mainly procedural) obligations that third-country nationals must fulfil when they reside in Greece. In accordance with Article 20(1), if they fail to observe these obligations, a fine of EUR 100 and, in case of recurrence, a fine of EUR 200 shall be imposed. Article 20(2) introduces another obligation, that of the timely departure of the migrant from the Greek territory. In particular, third-country nationals, who breach the deadline for voluntary departure under Article 22 of the aforementioned Law 3907/2011,[265] or in any other case reside not legally in the country for a period of time not exceeding thirty days, must pay a fine (it is a penalty of an administrative nature) whose amount will be four times the prescribed fee for an annual

265. Law 3907/2011 on the establishment of an Asylum Service, *supra*. Note that Law 3907/2011 adapted the domestic legislation Directive 2008/115/EC of the European Parliament and of the Council of 16 Dec. 2008 on common standards and procedures in Member States for returning illegally staying third-country nationals, O.J. L 348, 24.12.2008, p. 98. Article 22 of Law 3907/2011 provides that the period of voluntary departure can vary between seven and twenty-five days and is automatically granted, without requiring the submission of an application by the third-country national. At any rate, migrants may depart from the Greek territory even before the set deadline. This follows from the fact that migrants have a right to leave Greece at any time and they may not be prevented from doing so (it goes without saying only if they are in good standing and there is no outstanding arrest warrant or court judgment imposing criminal sanctions against them, etc.).

residence permit. If the stay exceeds thirty days, the amount to be paid will be eight times the annual residence permit fee.[266] However, there are certain categories of migrants, who, pursuant to Article 20(3), are exempt from the imposition of fines, including those under-aged and those having the status of spouse or parent of a citizen of the EU. Moreover, if it is proven that misleading or falsified documents or fraud were used in any way for being issued a residence permit, the third-country national in question shall be barred for five years from applying for a residence permit. Arguably, that the third-country national in question used illegal means to secure a residence permit could potentially be regarded as posing a threat to public order and/or to public security and his (re)application should be rejected on this ground.[267]

## §2. Sanctions Imposed on Employees of Public Authorities

*210.* According to Article 21(1) of Law 5038/2023, public authorities, legal entities governed by public law, local government organizations, utilities companies, social security institutions, etc., are required not to provide their services to third-country nationals, who are not in possession of a valid passport (or other travel documents) having an entry visa or in possession of a valid residence permit or who are not able to show that they have entered and reside legally in Greece. There are numerous exceptions to this prohibition, including the following two: (a) the duty of hospitals to disregard this prohibition, if there is an urgent need for hospitalization or childbirth and always in the case of children; and (b) illegally employed migrants, who lodge complaints or want to have recourse to the competent courts of justice and other relevant public authorities.[268] Should the employees of these public authorities violate the prohibition of Article 21, they are subject to disciplinary action and shall be punished, according to the provisions of the Penal Code, for breach of duty.[269]

266. For the amount of the various fees, *see* Art. 171 of Law 5038/2023.
267. Generally, *see* Art. 8 of Law 5038/2023.
268. *See* further Arts 83 and 86 of the aforementioned Law 4052/2012. Under Art. 83(2), aiding third-country nationals in filing a complaint shall in no way be considered assisting an illegally employed person to gain illegal entry and residence in Greece. Under Art. 86(1), illegally employed third-country nationals may, like any legally employed person, lodge a (civil) action before the competent court of justice in order to claim what is due to them (wages in arrears, compulsory social security contributions, etc.) and generally to assert their legal rights in accordance with the applicable Greek labour law and to execute court decisions against their employers. The latter applies even if a migrant worker has returned to or was forced to return to the country of origin (expulsion order).
269. Note that the relevant provision (Art. 259 of the Penal Code) requires the existence of *dolus malus*: 'An official/public servant, who intentionally violates the duties of his service in order to obtain for himself or another unlawful advantage or to harm the State or someone else, shall be punished with imprisonment for up to two years, if the criminal act committed is not more heavily punishable by another criminal provision.' Generally, on *dolus malus see* Anagnostopoulos and Magliveras, *Criminal Law in Greece*, *supra* n. 66, pp. 83 et seq., and on offences relating to public service, *see* Arts 235–263A of the Penal Code, and *Criminal Law in Greece*, *ibid.*, pp. 129 et seq.

## §3. Sanctions Imposed on the Employers of Migrant Workers

*211.* In accordance with Article 23(1) of Law 5038/2023, the recruitment and employment of third-country nationals is not permitted, if they do not fulfil the conditions for legal residence in Greece. Any employer who has violated this obligation shall face the penalties envisaged in the aforementioned Law 4052/2012 as well as any other sanctions provided for by the legislation (there is no mention of which these provisions are).[270] Equally, under Article 23(2), it is not allowed to recruit and employ third-country nationals, if their residence permit or entry visa does not give them the right of access to the labour market. Moreover, if the conclusion of the employment contract is a prerequisite for being granted the residence permit, the validity of the contract shall be based on the residence permit having been issued. It follows that the mere conclusion of a valid employment contract is not enough for the migrant worker to be considered to be in lawful employment.

*212.* In case Article 23(2) has been breached, Article 23(4) stipulates that in addition to the other sanctions provided for by the legislation (again, no mention is made of which the specific legislative instruments are), a fine of EUR 1,500 shall be imposed for each third-country national, who happens to be in legal residence but is illegally employed. If the victim is a minor, the Immigration Code considers that the employer has committed a very serious offence (felony) and, therefore, he shall be punished by confinement in a penitentiary of up to ten years and a monetary penalty ranging between EUR 10,000 and EUR 50,000.

*213.* Even harsher criminal penalties (confinement in a penitentiary and a monetary penalty of between EUR 50,000 and EUR 100,000) are envisaged if a crime coming into the ambit of Article 23(5) was committed in the following cases: (a) against a person who was younger than 15 years; (b) by using deceitful means; (c) the perpetrator was a close relative by blood or by marriage of the victim, or a foster parent, or a spouse, or someone to whom the upbringing of a minor had been entrusted, even temporarily; and (d) by a public employee (public servant) who, during the exercise of his duties or by exploiting his position and status, committed or participated in any way in such a criminal act. The literal interpretation of these provisions shows that they are not only related to employers but also to other categories of persons (relatives, custodians, public officials).

*214.* Once an irrevocable conviction has been delivered by the competent court of justice, the judgment is notified to the Secretary of the relevant Decentralized Administration, who must promptly revoke the operating licence of the store or business where the criminal act was committed for at least twelve months. In case circumstances so warrant it, the operating licence can be cancelled.

---

270. As explained *supra*, the nationality and the legal status of the employer (natural person, legal person, etc.) is irrelevant.

*215.* Article 23(8) of Law 5038/2023 places upon the employers of seasonal migrant workers the duty to secure them suitable accommodation. Should an inspection reveal that it was not provided or that the accommodation offered is not in compliance with the required health and safety standards, the employer shall be imposed a fine of EUR 1,500 and shall not be allowed to recall seasonal migrant workers (Articles 4 and 27 of Law 5038/2023) for a period of five years. It is not explained in the Immigration Code whether the fine of EUR 1,500 shall be imposed for each seasonal migrant worker or as a blanket fine for the whole business, in other words, irrespective of the number of workers with unsuitable accommodation. Finally, pursuant to Article 23(11), if the employer is a subcontractor, who violated the provisions of Article 23, and if the main contractor and any intermediate subcontractor have not fulfilled their obligations with due diligence, the main contractor and any intermediate subcontractor shall be subject, *inter alia*, to the sanctions of Article 23(8) and shall be obliged to pay, on the one hand, any compensation that was due to the seasonal migrant workers under Article 85 of Law 4052/2012, and, on the other hand, any overdue amounts owed to seasonal migrant in accordance with Articles 81 and 85 of Law 4052/2012.

*216.* It should be noted that, if the period of employment of irregular migrant workers is in dispute, they are considered to have been employed for a minimum period of three months, unless either the employer or the migrant himself proves otherwise. Under Article 83 of Law 4052/2012, illegally employed migrants have the right, like any legally employed worker, to submit (or consent to the submission on their behalf) any complaint which is provided for in the domestic legislation against their employer. Indeed, irregular migrants have a right to be informed about these rules and procedures.

*217.* In addition, Article 86 of Law 4052/2012 allows illegally employed third-country nationals, like any legally employed worker, to apply to the competent court of justice or to the competent public authority and claim what they are owed from salaries and wages. Generally speaking, they have every right to assert their privileges pursuant to the labour legislation. They also have the right to execute and enforce court judgments which were given against their employers; this right may be exercised even after they were repatriated to the country of origin, in case the court judgment was rendered at a later stage. To put it otherwise, the fact that they are no longer present in Greece does not operate to their detriment; on the contrary, they retain their civil claims against the employer. Moreover, pursuant to Article 89 of Law 4052/2012, those migrants who were employed under particularly abusive working conditions and who assist the competent law enforcement authorities in bringing criminal proceedings against their employers are entitled to apply to be issued a residence permit for humanitarian reasons.

*218.* Finally, the relevant domestic legislation on the principle of equal treatment at work (the aforementioned Law 4443/2016) lays down the imposition of fines and other sanctions on those who have violated it. As was mentioned *supra*, this is a principle of EU law. There are also other provisions envisaged in the legislation for the protection of equal treatment. In particular, those who have allegedly suffered from unequal treatment at work have access to a court of justice to submit their grievance (i.e., they are afforded judicial protection), they benefit from a reversal of the burden of proof, and they are also protected against countermeasures that have been taken against them.

## §4. Sanctions Imposed on Private Individuals, Including Third-Country Nationals

*219.* Article 24(1) of Law 5038/2023 provides that it is prohibited to rent immovable property to a third-country national, who does not possess a passport with an entry visa or a residence permit. Should this prohibition be breached, the Secretary of the competent Decentralized Administration shall impose an (administrative) fine between EUR 1,500 and EUR 3,000. Moreover, pursuant to Article 24(3), persons submitting incorrect declarations or certificates that are provided for in the Immigration Code as well as third-country nationals, who hold a residence permit but are employed or are engaged in an independent economic activity, without having the required residence permit or without being authorized to access the labour market, shall be fined the amount of EUR 150.

*220.* Far more severe penalties of a criminal nature are to be imposed, pursuant to Article 24(4) of Law 5038/2023, to whoever facilitates the entry of a third-country national into the Greek territory or facilitates his leaving it without having been through the checks and controls provided for in the aforementioned Article 5 of Law 5038/2023 (entering and leaving the Greek territory only from the official border crossing points). More specifically, enabling a third-country national to enter from an unauthorized border point is considered a very serious offence (felony) and is punishable by confinement in a penitentiary for up to ten years and a fine of at least EUR 20,000. In case it is proven that the perpetrator acted to enrich himself or was committing this offence by profession or by habit or if the crime was committed by two or more persons jointly (and therefore a criminal organization had been established), the penalty shall be confinement in a penitentiary for at least ten years and a fine of at least EUR 50,000. Arguably, the severity of these penalties is to deter the smuggling of immigrants into Greece, primarily through the Aegean Sea and the Greek/Turkish land borders.

*221.* According to Article 24(5) of Law 5038/2023, whoever (i.e., Greek national, EU citizen or foreigner) facilitates the illegal stay of a third-country national or hinders Police investigations to identify, arrest and expel him shall be punished by imprisonment between one and five years and a fine of at least EUR 5,000. If the perpetrator acted to enrich himself, the penalties would be doubled (imprisonment between two and five years and a fine of at least EUR 10,000).

*222.* Under Article 24(6) of Law 5038/2023, anyone who illegally possesses a travel document or uses another person's genuine passport to gain entry into the country faces imprisonment of between six months and five years as well as a fine of at least EUR 3,000. The same penalty shall apply to anyone who withholds a passport of another person or possesses or uses a false passport. Furthermore, Article 24(7) provides that the person who is in charge of a travel agency or anyone who submits on behalf of a third person to the competent public authority the necessary documents for the issuance of a travel document, even though they are not aware that they do not correspond to the identity of that person, shall be punished by a term of imprisonment between one and five years and a fine of at least EUR 10,000. The same penalties are threatened against the person on whose behalf the documents were submitted. Finally, if the act was committed by a travel agency, it shall face the administrative penalty of a three-month withdrawal of its operating licence and, in case of regression, permanent withdrawal (revocation) of the licence.

# Appendix

List of the categories and types of residence permits issued in Greece pursuant to Article 9 of the Immigration Code (Law 5038/2023)

1. *Residence permits for employment* (Category 'E')[271]
   1.1 Residence permit for high-skilled employment (EU Directive 2021/1883)[272] (residence permit type 'E.1')
   1.2 Residence permit for intra-corporate transfer (EU Directive 2014/66)[273] (residence permit type 'E.2')
   1.3 Residence permit for special purpose employment (residence permit type 'E.3')
   1.4 Residence permit for migrant workers who have been recalled from abroad (residence permit type 'E.4')
   1.5 Residence permit to holders of national entry visas for the purpose of seasonal work (residence permit type 'E.5')
   1.6 Residence permit for seasonal workers (residence permit type 'E.6')
2. *Right to residence permit and to employment to the holders of national long-stay visas* (category 'Z')
   2.1 Residence permit for digital nomads (residence permit type 'Z.1')
   2.2 Residence permit for the members of artistic groups (residence permit type 'Z.2')
   2.3 Residence permit for intellectual creators (residence permit type 'Z.3')
   2.4 Residence permit for third-country nationals moving from an undertaking established in another Member State of the European Union or of the European Economic Area for the purpose of providing a service (residence permit type 'Z.4')
   2.5 Residence permit for third-country nationals moving from an undertaking established in a third country for the purpose of providing a service (residence permit type 'Z.5'),
   2.6 Residence permit for leaders of organized tourism groups (residence permit type 'Z.6')

271. Note that the letters designating the various categories and types appear here as they are laid down in Law 5038/2023. The same applies to the titles of the various residence permits.
272. *See* Table of EU legislation.
273. *See* Table of EU legislation.

- 2.7 Residence permit for third-country nationals applying for admission to prepare (training) for sport events (residence permit type 'Z.7')
- 2.8 Residence permit for higher education students participating in internship programmes for which they are compensated (residence permit type 'Z.8')
- 2.9 Residence permit for Australian citizens participating in the youth mobility programme under the Memorandum of Understanding between Greece and Australia (Work and Holiday Visa) (residence permit type 'Z.9')[274]
- 2.10 Residence permit for flying, technical and administrative personnel entering the Greek territory to participate in forest fire fighting during the anti-fire season (residence permit type 'Z.10')
- 2.11 Residence permit for the scholars of the American Educational Foundation of Greece (Fulbright Greece Foundation) (residence permit type 'Z.11')
- 2.12 Residence permit for third-country nationals applying for admission to study or to gain acquainted with: (a) the life of monks in Mount Athos;[275] or (b) the monastic life – monasticism (residence permit type 'Z.12'),

3. *Residence permits for family reasons* (category 'O')
   - 3.1 Residence permit for third-country nationals for family reunification in accordance with Directive 2003/86/EC,[276] incorporated into Greek law under Presidential Decree 131/2006[277] (FEK 2006 Issue A' No. 143) (residence permit type 'O.1')
   - 3.2 Independent (separate) residence permit for family members pursuant to Directive 2003/86/EC[278] and for family members of Greek citizens who meet the conditions for obtaining a separate residence permit (residence permit type 'O.2')
   - 3.3 Residence card of the family members of a Greek citizen (spouse, parents, children, parents and siblings of under-aged Greek nationals) (residence permit type 'O.3')
4. *Residence permits for investment purposes* (category 'B')
   - 4.1 Residence permit for strategic investors (residence permit type 'B1')
   - 4.2 Residence permit for investment purposes through the establishment and operation of an undertaking/company (natural persons, members of the Board of Directors, shareholders – equity partners) (residence permit type 'B2')
   - 4.3 Residence permit for executives of companies established in Greece and of subsidiaries of foreign companies which are established in Greece and

274. Ratified under Law 4353/2015, FEK 2015 Issue A' No. 173.
275. Mount Athos (also called *Agion Oros* (Holy Mountain)) is a male monastic society located in Northern Greece. It is a self-administered region which is expressly protected under Art. 105 of the Constitution.
276. *See* Table of EU legislation.
277. *See* Table of Greek legislation.
278. *See* Table of EU legislation.

engaged in commercial activities (shareholders – equity partners, members of the Board of Directors, managers, legal representatives) (residence permit type 'B3')

4.4 Residence permit for financial investments (residence permit type 'B4')

4.5 Residence permit for investors in real estate (permanent investor residence permit) (residence permit type 'B5')

5. *Residence permits for educational purposes* (category 'H')

5.1 Residence permit for the purpose of studies pursuant to Law 4666/2020 amending Law 4251/2014 on the adaptation of Greek legislation to Directive 2016/801 of the European Parliament and of the Council of 11 May 2016 on the conditions of entry and residence of third-country nationals for the purpose of research, studies, traineeships, voluntary service, pupil exchange schemes or educational projects and the employment of au pairs without remuneration[279] (residence permit type 'H.1')

5.2 Residence permit for the purpose of voluntary service pursuant to EU Directive 2016/801 (residence permit type 'H.2')

5.3 Residence permit for the purpose of research according to EU Directive 2016/801 (residence permit type 'H.3')

5.4 National entry visa allowing temporary stay for traineeship under EU Directive 2016/801 (residence permit type 'H.4')

5.5 Residence permit for vocational training (attending colleges, vocational training institutes, vocational training schools and lifelong learning centres) (residence permit type 'H.5')

5.6 National entry visa allowing the residence of third-country nationals who work in an undertaking, which is established in a third state or in another Member State of the European Union or of the European Union Economic Area, and who participate in study programmes offered by colleges, which exclusively provide studies on the basis of accreditation (validation) agreements and franchising agreements with foreign higher educational institutions, which are recognized by the competent authorities of the state in which they are established (residence permit type 'H.6')

5.7 Residence permit for scholarship holders as well as for the participants in special programmes (e.g., ERASMUS as well as Greek State Scholarships Foundation (IKY) scholars) (residence permit type 'H.7')

5.8 National entry visa allowing the residence of students of foreign higher educational institutions, who participate in summer study programmes in accordance with Article 90 of Law 4692/2020[280] (residence permit type 'H.8')

5.9 Residence permit for attending the schools and the special schools of the Greek Armed Forces, of the State Security Forces or the Merchant Marine academies and schools, schools for the training of pilots, engineers and cabin crew members, the Athonite Ecclesiastical Academy of

279. *See* Tables of Greek and EU legislation.

280. *See* Table of Greek legislation.

Mount Athos, musical educational institutions, Greek language teaching centres or similar entities of higher education (residence permit type 'H.9')

5.10 Residence permit for obtaining a medical speciality ('residency programmes') (residence permit type 'H.10')

6. *Residence permits for humanitarian and exceptional reasons* (category 'A')

6.1 Ad hoc residence permit for humanitarian grounds, in particular to: (a) third-country nationals who are victims and essential witnesses of crime; victims of domestic violence; victims of a crime with racist characteristics, those suffering from severe health problems; victims of work accidents; (b) third-country nationals who attend a legally approved mental addiction treatment programme; and (c) third-country nationals, who by risking their lives performed acts of social virtue and acts of solidarity that promote the values of humanism (residence permit type 'A.1')

6.2 Residence permit for the victims of trafficking in human beings, who are subject to the provisions of the Palermo Protocol, ratified by Law 3875/2010,[281] and who do not come under the provisions of Articles 135 to 142 of Law 5038/2023 (residence permit type 'A.2')

6.3 Residence permit for third-country nationals who were employed either on particularly abusive terms or were employed despite being minors, in accordance with Article 89 of Law 4052/2012[282] (residence permit type 'A.3')

6.4 Residence permit for: (a) adults, who are unable to take care of their affairs due to health reasons, or minors, who are proven to be in need of protection measures and are hosted by public benefit institutions, provided that their return to a safe environment is impossible; (b) minors whose custody has been awarded by virtue of the judgment of a Greek court or a foreign court, which is recognized by the Greek authorities, to a Greek family or to a family of third-country nationals with legal residence in Greece or for whom adoption proceedings before the Greek authorities are pending; and (c) minors who have been placed with a foster family either by court order or on the basis of a written contract between the natural parents or the guardian or the institution having custody of the minor with the foster parents (residence permit type 'A.4')

6.5 Residence permit for minors staying in boarding schools, operating under the supervision of the competent ministries (residence permit type 'A.5')

6.6 Residence permit for third-country nationals for exceptional reasons (residence permit type 'A.6')

6.7 Residence permit for victims of trafficking in human beings or migrant smuggling under EU Directive 2004/81[283] (residence permit type 'A.7')

281. *Ibid.*
282. *Ibid.*
283. *See* Table of EU legislation.

7. *Long-term residence permits* (category 'M');
   7.1 Long-term residence permit pursuant to Council Directive 2003/109/EC of 25 November 2003 concerning the status of third-country nationals who are long-term residents[284] (residence permit type 'M.1')
   7.2 Residence permit of ten-year validity (residence permit type 'M.2')
8. *Residence permit for citizens of the European Union*
   Residence permit for the citizens of the European Union and the members of their family, according to Directive 2004/38/EC of the European Parliament and of the Council of 29 April 2004 on the right of citizens of the Union and their family members to move and reside freely within the territory of the Member States amending Regulation (EEC) No. 1612/68 and repealing Directives 64/221/EEC, 68/360/EEC, 72/194/EEC, 73/148/EEC, 75/34/EEC, 75/35/EEC, 90/364/EEC, 90/365/EEC and 93/96/EEC,[285] which was incorporated into the Greek legislation by Presidential Decree 106/2007[286] (category 'N')
9. *Residence permits for other reasons* (category 'I')
   9.1 Residence permit that serves the public (State) interest (residence permit type 'I.1'),
   9.2 Residence permit for: (a) adults, who are over twenty years of age, children of members of the diplomatic, administrative and technical staff of a diplomatic mission, if they live with their parents; (b) adults, who are over twenty years of age, children of consular officers and special consular officials who serve in Greece; and (c) dependent family members, who are first-degree relatives in the ascending line of the members of the diplomatic and administrative and technical staff of diplomatic missions, as well as of consular posts officers and special consular officials who serve in Greece (residence permit type 'I.2')
   9.3 Residence permit for those employed as private servants of members of diplomatic missions, in accordance with Article 1(8) of the 1961 Vienna Convention 'On Diplomatic Relations',[287] ratified by Legislative Decree 503/1970,[288] who are abroad and are invited to Greece (residence permit type 'I.3')
   9.4 Residence permit to receive medical care, nursing care and palliative care (residence permit type 'I.4')
   9.5 Residence permit for Canadian citizens participating in the Youth Mobility Programme under the Agreement between Greece and Canada (Work and Holiday Visa), ratified by Law 4091/2012[289] (residence permit type 'I.5')
   9.6 Residence permits for foreign press correspondents (residence permit type 'I.6')

284. *Ibid.*
285. *Ibid.*
286. *See* Table of Greek legislation.
287. *See* Table of International Treaties.
288. *See* Table of Greek legislation.
289. *Ibid.*

9.7 Residence permit: (a) for the study or acquaintance with the Mount Athos monastic life; or (b) for the acquaintance with monastic life – monasticism (residence permit type 'I.7')

9.8 Residence permit for third-country nationals with sufficient subsistence resources (residence permit type 'I.8')

10. *Residence permits for purposes of international protection and temporary protection (category 'P')*

10.1 Residence permit for refugees (residence permit type 'P.1'),

10.2 Residence permit for a beneficiary of subsidiary protection (residence permit type 'P.2')

10.3 Residence permits for temporary protection (residence permit type 'P.3')

11. Residence permits for 'omogeneis' (category 'Y')

11.1 Residence permit for 'omogeneis' if there is no possibility to be included in the regulatory framework for 'omogeneis' coming from Albania, Turkey or countries of the former USSR (residence permit type 'Y.1')

11.2 Residence permit for 'omogeneis' coming from Albania, Turkey and the former U.S.S.R. (residence permit type 'Y.2')

11.3 Residence permit of family members of 'omogeneis' from the countries of the former U.S.S.R. (residence permit type 'Y.3')

11.4 Special certificate of legal residence pursuant to Article 16(4) of Law 5038/2023 (residence permit type 'X') [it concerns those third-country nationals, whose request for renewal of residence permit was rejected or the issued residence permit was revoked and, pending their action of annulment against these decisions, their execution has been suspended by the competent administrative court of justice]

# Table of Legislation

### 1. Greek legislation (laws – legislative/presidential decrees – ministerial decisions) (in chronological order)

Law 4310/1929, Establishment and movement of aliens in Greece, police controls, passports, deportations and displacements, FEK 1929 Issue A' No. 237
Constitution of the Hellenic Republic (1975), FEK 2019 Issue A' No. 211
Law 1245/1982, Ratification of the Agreement between the Hellenic Republic and the Arab Republic of Egypt on exemption of Greek workers in Egypt and Egyptian workers in Greece from charges required for the granting and/or renewal of work permits signed in Cairo on 18 April 1981, FEK 1982 Issue A' No. 45
Law 1264/1982, For the Democratization of the Trade Union Movement and Securing Workers' Trade Union Freedoms, FEK 1982 Issue A' No. 79
Law 1705/1987, Ratification of Protocol No. 7 to the Convention for the Protection of Human Rights and Fundamental Freedoms, FEK 1987 Issue A' No. 89
Law 1782/1988, Ratification of the Convention against Torture and Other Cruel, Inhuman or Degrading Treatment or Punishment, FEK 1988 Issue A' No. 116
Law 1975/1991, Entry, exit, stay, employment, deportation of aliens, procedure for recognition of foreign refugees and other provisions, FEK 1991 Issue A' No. 184
Law 2289/1995, Search, exploration and exploitation of hydrocarbons and other provisions, FEK 1995, Issue A' No. 27
Law 2514/1997, Ratification: (1) of the Agreement between the Governments of the States of the Benelux Economic Union, the Federal Republic of Germany and the French Republic on the gradual abolition of checks at their common borders, (2) of the Convention implementing the above Agreement between the same Member States, (3) of the Protocols and Agreements of accession to the above Agreements: of the Italian Republic, the Kingdom of Spain, the Portuguese Republic, the Hellenic Republic, the Republic of Austria, the Republic of Finland, the Kingdom of Denmark and the Kingdom of Sweden, together with their final acts, minutes, declarations and joint declarations, FEK 1997 Issue A' No. 140
Law 2690/1999, Ratification of the Code of Administrative Procedure and other provisions, FEK 1999 Issue A' No. 45
Law 2800/2000, Restructuring of the Ministry of Public Order, establishment of the Hellenic Police Headquarters and other provisions, FEK 2000 Issue A' No. 41
Law 2910/2001, Entry and residence of aliens in the Greek territory, acquisition of Greek citizenship by naturalization and other provisions, FEK 2001 Issue A' No. 91

**Table of Legislation**

Law 3003/2002, Ratification of the Statute of the International Criminal Law, FEK 2002 Issue A' No. 75

Law 3068/2002, Compliance of the Greek public administration with the decisions of the courts of justice, FEK 2002 Issue A' No. 274

Law 3251/2004, European Arrest Warrant, amendment of Law 2928/2001 on criminal organisations and other provisions, FEK 2004 Issue A' No. 127

Law 3284/2004, On the ratification of the Code on Hellenic Nationality, FEK 2004 Issue A' No. 217

Law 3386/2005, Entry, residence and social integration of third-country nationals into the Greek territory, FEK 2005 Issue A' No. 212

Law 3536/2007, Special arrangements for immigration policy issues and other matters falling into the competence of the Ministry of the Interior, Public Administration and Decentralization, FEK 2007 Issue A' No. 42

Law 3671/2008, Ratification of the Treaty on European Union, the Treaty on the Functioning of the European Union, and certain other relevant acts, FEK 2008 Issue A' No. 129

Law 3692/2008, Ratification of the Agreement between the Government of the Hellenic Republic and the Council of Ministers of Albania for the protection and assistance of children victims of trafficking, FEK 2008 Issue A' No. 173

Law 3838/2010, Current provisions for the Greek citizenship and for the political participation of 'omogeneis' and lawfully resident immigrants, and other provisions, FEK 2010 Issue A' No. 49

Law 3875/2010, Ratification and application of the United Nations Convention against Transnational Organized Crime and of the three Protocols to it and relevant provisions, FEK 2010 A' No. 158.

Law 3907/2011, Establishment of an Asylum Service and a First Reception Service, adaptation of Greek legislation to the provisions of Directive 2008/115/EC 'regarding the common rules and procedures in the member states for the return of illegally staying third-country nationals' and other provisions, FEK 2011 Issue A' No. 7

Law 3948/2011 on the adaptation of the domestic law to the provisions of the Statute of the International Criminal Court, adopted by Law 3003/2002, FEK 2011 Issue A' No. 71

Law 4052/2012, Legislation falling into the competence of the Ministries of Health and Social Solidarity and Labour and Social Security for the implementation of the law 'Approval of the Draft Financial Facility Agreements between the European Financial Stability Facility (EFSF), the Hellenic Republic and the Bank of Greece, the Draft Memorandum of Understanding between the Hellenic Republic, the European Commission and the Bank of Greece and other urgent provisions for the reduction of the public sector debt and saving the national economy' and other provisions, FEK 2012 Issue A' No. 41

Law 4091/2012, Ratification of the Agreement between the Hellenic Republic and Canada concerning youth mobility, FEK 2012 Issue A' No. 219

Law 4216/2013, Council of Europe Convention on Action against Trafficking in Human Beings, FEK 2013 Issue A' No. 266

Law 4244/2014, Transposition into Greek law of Council Directive 2013/1/EU of 20 December 2012 amending Directive 93/109/EC regarding detailed arrangements for the exercise of the right to stand for election in the European Parliament elections by citizens of the Union residing in a Member State of which they are not nationals, and amendment of Law 2196/1994, and other provisions, FEK 2014 Issue A' No. 60

Law 4251/2014, Immigration and Social Integration Code, FEK 2014 Issue A' No. 80

Law 4332/2015, Amendment of the provisions of the Greek Citizenship Code – Amendment of Law 4251/2014 for the adaptation of the Greek legislation to the directives of the European Parliament and of the Council 2011/98/EU regarding the single procedure for submitting an application for the granting of a single residence permit to citizens of third countries and of work in the territory of a Member State and on a common set of rights for workers from third countries legally residing in a Member State and 2014/36/EU on the conditions of entry and residence of citizens of third countries for the purpose of seasonal work and other provisions, FEK 2015 Issue A' No. 76

Law 4353/2015, Ratification of the Memorandum of Understanding between the Government of the Hellenic Republic and the Government of Australia on the regulation of issues relating to entry visas for the transfer of young people (Work and Holiday Visa), FEK 2015 Issue A' No. 173.

Law 4375/2016, Organization and operation of the Asylum Service, the Appeals Authority, the Reception and Identification Service, the establishment of a General Secretariat for Reception, adaptation of Greek legislation to the provisions of Directive 2013/32/EU of the European Parliament and of the Council 'on common procedures for granting and withdrawing international protection (recast)' (L 180/29.6.2013), provisions on the employment of beneficiaries of international protection and other provisions, FEK 2016 Issue A' No. 51

Law 4443/2016, (i) Incorporation of Directive 2000/43/EC on the implementation of the principle of equal treatment of persons regardless of racial or ethnic origin, of Directive 2000/78/EC on the establishment of a general framework for equal treatment in employment and work, and of Directive 2014/54/EU on measures that facilitate the exercise of workers' rights in the context of the free movement of workers; (ii) Taking the necessary measures to comply with Articles 22, 23, 30, 31(1), 32 and 34 of Regulation 596/2014 on market abuse and the repeal of Directive 2003/6/EC of the European Parliament and of the Council and of Commission Directives 2003/124/EC, 2003/125 EC and 2004/72/EC and incorporation of Directive 2014/57/EU on criminal sanctions for market abuse and Implementing Directive 2015/2392; (iii) Incorporation of Directive 2014/62 on the protection of the euro and other currencies against counterfeiting by criminal law, and replacing Council Framework Decision 2000/383/JHA, and (iv) Establishment of a National Mechanism to Investigate Incidents of Arbitrariness by the security forces and the employees of detention centers, and other provisions, FEK 2016 Issue A' No. 232

Law 4540/2018, Adaptation of Greek legislation to the provisions of Directive 2013/33/EU of the Parliament and of the Council of 26 June 2013, regarding the provisions for the reception of applicants for international protection (recast, L

180/96/29.6.2013) and other provisions – Amendment of Law 4251/2014 for the adaptation of Greek legislation to Council Directive 2014/66/EU of 15 May 2014 regarding the entry and residence conditions of third-country nationals in the context of intra-company transfers – Amendment of asylum procedures and other provisions, FEK 2018 Issue A' No. 91

Law 4620/2019, Ratification of the Code of Criminal Procedure, FEK 2019 Issue A' No. 96

Law 4622/2019, Organization, operation and transparency of the Government, government bodies and central public administration, FEK 2019 Issue A' No. 133

Law 4636/2019 on International Protection and other provisions, FEK 2019 Issue A' No. 169

Law 4652/2020, Arrangements for the withdrawal of the United Kingdom from the European Union and other provisions, FEK 2020 Issue A' No. 9

Law 4666/2020, Amendment of Law 4251/2014 on the adaptation of Greek legislation to Directive (EU) 2016/801 of the European Parliament and of the Council of 11 May 2016 regarding the entry and residence conditions of third-country nationals for the purpose of research, studies, internships, voluntary service, student exchanges or training programs and the employment of domestic unpaid assistants (au pair), FEK 2020 Issue A' No. 35.

Law 4686/2020, Improvement of the immigration legislation, amendment of provisions in Law 4636/2019, in Law 4375/2016 and in Law 4251/2014, and other provisions, FEK 2020 Issue A' No. 96

Law 4689/2020, Incorporation into Greek legislation of Directives (EU) 2016/800, 2017/1371, 2017/541, 2016/1919, 2014/57/EU, ratification of the Memorandum of Administrative Cooperation between the Ministry of Justice of the Hellenic Republic and the Ministry of Justice and Public Order of the Republic of Cyprus, amendments to Law 3663/2008 so as to implement Regulation (EU) 2018/1727 and other provisions, FEK 2020 Issue A' No. 103

Law 4692/2020, Upgrading of schools and other provisions, FEK 2020 Issue A' No. 111

Law 4808/2021, On the protection of work – Establishment of the independent administrative authority 'Labour Inspectorate' – Ratification of Convention No. 190 concerning the elimination of violence and harassment in the world of work of the International Labour Organization – Ratification of Convention No. 187 concerning the promotional framework for occupational safety and health of the International Labour Organization – Incorporation of Directive (EU) 2019/1158 of the European Parliament and of the Council of 20 June 2019 on work-life balance, other provisions of the Ministry of Labour and Social Security and other emergency provisions, FEK 2021 Issue A' No. 101

Law 4819/2021, Integrated framework for waste management – Incorporation of Directives 2018/851 and 2018/852 of the European Parliament and of the Council of 30 May 2018 amending Directive 2008/98/EC on waste and Directive 94/62/EC on packaging and packaging waste – Framework for the organization of the Hellenic Recycling Agency – Provisions on plastic products and the protection of the natural environment – Spatial-urban, energy and related emergency regulations, FEK 2021 Issue A' No. 129

Law 4825/2021, Reform of procedures for deportations and returns of third-country nationals, attracting investors and digital nomads, issues of residence permits and procedures for granting international protection, provisions of the competence of the Ministry of Migration and Asylum and of the Ministry of Citizen Protection, and other urgent provisions, FEK 2021 Issue A' No. 157

Law 4864/2021, Strategic investments and improvement of the investment environment through the acceleration of processes in private and strategic investments, creating a framework for technology companies and other urgent provisions for development, FEK 2021 Issue A' No. 237

Law 4939/2022, Ratification of a Code of Legislation on reception, international protection of third-country nationals and stateless persons, and temporary protection in case of mass influx of displaced aliens, FEK 2022 Issue A' No. 111

Law 4957/2022, New Horizons in Higher Education Institutions: Strengthening the quality, functionality and connection of Higher Education Institutions with society, and other provisions, FEK 2022 Issue A' No. 141

Law 4959/2022, Ratification of the Memorandum of Understanding between the Government of the Hellenic Republic and the Government of the People's Republic of Bangladesh on Migration and Mobility, FEK 2022 Issue A' No. 144

Law 4960/2022, National guardianship system and accommodation framework for unaccompanied minors and other provisions pertaining to the Ministry of Migration and Asylum, FEK 2022 Issue A' No. 145.

Law 4962/2022, Upgrading police training, reforming the framework of organization and operation of the Academy of Greek Police Officers and other regulations of the Ministry of Citizen Protection, FEK 2022 Issue A' No. 148

Law 4978/2022, Ratification of the Public Revenue Collection Code, FEK 2022 Issue A' No. 190

Law 5007/2022, Integrated System for the Provision of Alleviative Care, Arrangements to Respond to the COVID-19 Pandemic and to Protect Public Health, and Other Emergency Arrangements, FEK 2022 Issue A' No. 241

Law 5009/2023, Ratification of the Agreement between the Government of the Hellenic Republic and the Government of the Arab Republic of Egypt on the Employment of Seasonal workers in the Agricultural Sector, FEK 2023 Issue A' No. 7

Law 5038/2023, Code of Immigration, FEK 2023 Issue A' No. 81

Law 5078/2023, Reform of occupational insurance, rationalization of the insurance legislation, pension arrangements, appointment system for and recruitment of teachers in the public employment service, and other provisions, FEK 2023 Issue A' No. 21

Law 5079/2023, Organizational and procedural provisions on development, interventions on enhancement of the fair developmental transition and other urgent provisions, FEK 2023 Issue A' No. 215

Law 5089/2024, Equality in civil marriage, amendment of the Civil Code and other provisions, FEK 2024 Issue A' No. 27

Law 5100/2024, Transposition of Directive (EU) 2022/2523 of the Council of 14 December 2022 on ensuring a global minimum level of taxation for multinational enterprise groups and large-scale domestic groups in the European Union (Pillar II) and other urgent provisions, FEK 2024 Issue A' No. 49

## Table of Legislation

Law 5108/2024, Consolidation of the first instance of jurisdiction, spatial restructuring of civil and criminal justice courts and other provisions, FEK 2024 Issue A' No. 65

Law 5130/2024, Strengthening of the control system for the Asset Declarations and the Declarations of Financial Interests envisaged in Law 5026/2023 – Placement of a foreign minor in an institution, in a child protection structure or in a foster family – Reopening of final court judgments due to a final decision of the European Court of Human Rights – Harmonization with Law 4624/2019 on the use of information by the Joint Investigation Teams to be applied during the execution of a European Investigation Order – Other provisions, FEK 2024 Issue A' No. 127

Law 5162/2024, Income support measures, tax incentives for innovation and business transformations and other provisions, FEK 2024 Issue A' No. 198

Legislative Decree 53/1974, On the ratification of the Convention which was signed in Rome on 4 November 1950 'for the protection of the human rights and the fundamental freedoms' as well as of the Additional Protocol of Paris of 20 March 1952, FEK 1974 Issue A' No. 256.

Presidential Decree 503/1985, Codification of the Code of Civil Procedure, FEK 1985 Issue A' No. 182

Presidential Decree 18/1989, Codification of legislation provisions on the Council of State, FEK 1989 Issue A' No. 8

Presidential Decree 233/2003, Protection and assistance according to Article 12 of Law 3064/2002 (FEK 2002 Issue A' No. 248) to victims of crimes of Articles 323, 323A, 323B, 348A, 349, 351 and 351A of the Penal Code, and Articles 87(5) and (6) and 88 of Law 3386/2005, FEK 2003 Issue A' No. 204

Presidential Decree 131/2006, Harmonization of the Greek legislation to Directive 2003/86/EC relating to the right of family reunification, FEK 2006 Issue A' No. 143

Presidential Decree 106/2007, Free movement and residence in the Greek territory of the citizens of the European Union and the members of their families, FEK 2007 Issue A' No. 135

Presidential Decree 38/2010 on the adaptation of the Greek legislation to Directive 2005/36/EC regarding the recognition of professional qualifications, FEK 2010 Issue A' No. 78

Presidential Decree 114/2010, Establishment of a uniform procedure for the recognition of refugee status or beneficiary of subsidiary protection for foreigners and stateless persons in compliance with Council Directive 2005/85/EC 'on minimum standards on procedures in Member States for granting and withdrawing refugee status', FEK 2010 Issue A' No. 195

Presidential Decree 113/2013, Establishment of a uniform procedure for granting refugee status or beneficiary of subsidiary protection to foreigners and stateless persons in compliance with Council Directive 2005/85/EC 'on minimum standards on procedures in Member States for granting and withdrawing refugee status' (L 326/13.12.2005) and other provisions, FEK 2013 Issue A' No. 146

Presidential Decree 123/2016, Reconstitution and renaming of the Ministry of Administrative Reform and E-Governance, re-establishment of the Ministry of Tourism, establishment of the Ministry of Migration Policy and the Ministry of Digital Policy, Telecommunications and Information, renaming of the Ministry of

Interior and Administrative Restructuring, the Ministry of Economy, Development and Tourism, and the Ministry of Infrastructure, Transport and Networks, FEK 2016 Issue A' No. 208

Presidential Decree 80/2022, Code of Individual Labour Law, FEK 2022 Issue A' No. 222

Joint Ministerial Decision 23443/2011, Determination of the type of residence permit granted to third-country nationals, spouses of EU citizens or Greek nationals, with whom they maintain a stable relationship which is duly proven, FEK 2011 Issue B' No. 2225

Decision of the Minister of Migration Policy 18951/22.6.2018 on the determination of the documents of certain date proving the seven years of continuous residence in the country of a third-country national who applies for a residence permit for exceptional reasons, FEK 2018 Issue B' No. 2487

Joint Ministerial Decision of the Minister of Citizen Protection and the Minister of Migration and Asylum 4000/1/113-a' of 19 October 2020, Designation of competent authorities to issue residence documents to the citizens of the United Kingdom and their family members, as well as more specific issues for the implementation of the Agreement on the withdrawal of the United Kingdom from the European Union, FEK 2020 Issue B' No. 4610

Decision No. 374365/2021 of the Minister of Migration and Asylum, FEK 2021 Issue B' No. 5242

Decision No. 674588/2022 of the Minister of Migration and Asylum, FEK 2022 Issue B' No. 5801

Joint Ministerial Decision 716659/2022, Application of Law 4959/2022 'Ratification of the Memorandum of Understanding between the Government of the Hellenic Republic and the Government of the People's Republic of Bangladesh on Migration and Mobility', FEK 2022 Issue B' No. 6271

Joint Ministerial Decision 788502/2023, Provision of legal aid to applicants for international protection, FEK 2023 Issue B' No. 42

Joint Ministerial Decision 538595/2023, Determination of third countries which are deemed to be safe and producing the national catalogue in accordance with Article 91 of 4939/2022, FEK 2023 Issue B' No. 7063

Decision of the Minister of Minister for Migration and Asylum 118654/2024, Determination of the form, content and procedure for the submission of applications, in accordance with the provisions of Article 176(12) of Law 5038/2023, and the way third-country nationals communicate with the competent services in accordance with the provisions of Article 176(16) of Law 5038/2023, FEK 2024 Issue B' No. 81.

Ministerial Decision 75147/2024, Determination of the documents proving the seven-year continuous residence in the country of a third-country national applying for a residence permit for exceptional reasons, as well as evidence of parental relationship between a third-country national and a minor, in accordance with paragraphs 5 and 6 of Article 134 of Law 5038/2023, FEK 2024 Issue B' No. 1596

Ministerial Decision 75166/2024, Redesignation of the competent authority for issuing the residence permits provided for in the provisions of Article 100 of Law

5038/2023 as well as the regulation of more specific matters for the issuance of these residence permits, FEK 2024 Issue B' No. 1596

Joint Ministerial Decision 95391/2024, Determination of the supporting documents, per category of national entry visa, and of the required documentation for the issuance and renewal of residence permits, in accordance with the provisions of Law 5038/2023, FEK 2024 Issue B' No. 1807

Decision of the Minister of Labour and Social Security 25058/2024 of 29 March 2024, Establishment of a minimum salary and a minimum daily wage for employees and craftsmen throughout the country, FEK 2024 Issue B' No. 1974Joint Ministerial Decision 133226/2024, Determination of the documents for the application of Article 27(1) of Law 5038/2023, FEK 2024 Issue B' No. 2626

Joint Ministerial Decision 133692/2024, Determination of the risks and benefits to be covered in order to issue full health insurance for third-country nationals applying for or renewing a residence permit and being insured by private insurance companies, FEK 2024 Issue B' No. 2724

Joint Ministerial Decision 41835/2024, Determination of the health and safety standards for the accommodation provided to third-country nationals who are seasonal workers. Procedures for supervision and the infliction of penalties – Adaptation to Article 5(1)(c), Article 6(1)(c) and Article 20 of Directive 2014/36/EU of the European Parliament and of the Council of 26 February 2014 on the conditions of entry and residence of third-country nationals for the purpose of seasonal work (L 94), FEK 2024 Issue B' No. 4577.

Joint Ministerial Decision 225679/2024, Determination of the amount and ways of proving the availability of sufficient resources provided for in the provisions of Law 5038/2023 and in other regulations, as well as the amount and ways of proving the required income for the application of the provisions of Articles 84 and 144 of Law 5038/2023, FEK 2024, Issue B' No. 5223

Decision 272153/2024, Amendment and completion of Joint Ministerial Decision 95391/2024 'Determination of the supporting documents, per category of national entry visa, and of the required documentation for the issuance and renewal of residence permits, in accordance with the provisions of Law 5038/2023', FEK 2024, Issue B' No. 6201

## 2. European Union legislation and other documents (in chronological order)

Charter of the Fundamental Rights in the European Union (2000)

Council Directive 2000/43/EC of 29 June 2000 implementing the principle of equal treatment between persons irrespective of racial or ethnic origin, O.J. L 180, 19.7.2000, p. 22

Council Directive 2000/78/EC of 27 November 2000 establishing a general framework for equal treatment in employment and occupation, O.J. L 303, 2.12.2000, p. 16

Council Directive 2001/55/EC of 20 July 2001 on minimum standards for giving temporary protection in the event of a mass influx of displaced persons and on measures promoting a balance of efforts between Member States in receiving such persons and bearing the consequences thereof, O.J. L 212, 7.8.2001, p. 12

Council Regulation (EC) No. 1030/2002 of 13 June 2002 laying down a uniform format for residence permits for third-country nationals, O.J. L 157, 15.6.2002, p. 1

Council Framework Decision of 13 June 2002 (2002/584/JHA) on the European arrest warrant and the surrender procedures between Member States, O.J. L 190, 18.7.2002, p. 1

Council Directive 2003/86/EC of 22 September 2003 on the right to family reunification, O.J. L 251, 3.10.2003, p. 12

Council Directive 2003/109/EC of the Council of 25 November 2003 concerning the status of third-country nationals who are long-term residents, O.J. L 16, 23.1.2004, p. 44

Directive 2004/38/EC of the European Parliament and of the Council of 29 April 2004 on the right of citizens of the Union and their family members to move and reside freely within the territory of the Member States amending Regulation (EEC) No. 1612/68 and repealing Directives 64/221/EEC, 68/360/EEC, 72/194/EEC, 73/148/EEC, 75/34/EEC, 75/35/EEC, 90/364/EEC, 90/365/EEC and 93/96/EEC, O.J. L 158, 30.4.2004, p. 77

Regulation (EC) 883/2004 of the European Parliament and of the Council of 29 April 2004 on the coordination of social security systems, O.J. L 166, 30.4.2004, p.1

Council Directive 2004/81/EC of 29 April 2004 on the residence permit issued to third-country nationals who are victims of trafficking in human beings or who have been the subject of an action to facilitate illegal immigration, who cooperate with the competent authorities, O.J. L 261, 6.8.2004, p. 19

Council Regulation (EC) No. 2007/2004 of 26 October 2004 establishing a European Agency for the Management of Operational Cooperation at the External Borders of the Member States of the European Union, O.J. L 349, 25.11.2004, p. 1

Agreement between the European Community and the Republic of Albania on the readmission of persons residing without authorisation – Declarations, O.J. L 124, 17.5.2005, p. 22

Directive 2005/36/EC of the European Parliament and of the Council of 7 September 2005 on the recognition of professional qualifications, O.J. L 255, 30.9.2005, p. 22

Agreement between the European Community and the Russian Federation on the facilitation of the issuance of visas to the citizens of the European Union and the Russian Federation, O.J. L 129, 17.5.2007, p. 27

Agreement between the European Community and the former Yugoslav Republic of Macedonia on the readmission of persons residing without authorisation – Joint Declarations, O.J. L 334, 19.12.2007, p. 7

Council Regulation (EC) 380/2008 of 18 April 2008 amending Regulation (EC) No. 1030/2002 laying down a uniform format for residence permits for third-country nationals, O.J. L 115, 29. 4.2008, p. 1

Directive 2008/115/EC of the European Parliament and of the Council of 16 December 2008 on common standards and procedures in Member States for returning illegally staying third-country nationals, O.J. L 348, 24.12.2008, p. 98

## Table of Legislation

Council of the European Union, European Pact on Migration and Asylum, 13440/08, Brussels, 24 September 2008

Directive 2009/52/EC of the European Parliament and of the Council of 18 June 2009 providing for minimum standards on sanctions and measures against employers of illegally staying third-country nationals, O.J. L 168, 30.6.2009, p. 24

Regulation (EC) No. 810/2009 of the European Parliament and of the Council of 13 July 2009 establishing a Community Code on Visas (Visa Code), O.J. L 243, 15.9.2009, p. 1

Commission Recommendation of 29 October 2009 on the use of the International Standard Classification of Occupations (ISCO-08), O.J. L 292, 10.11.2009, p. 31.

Directive 2011/51/EU of the European Parliament and of the Council of 11 May 2011 amending Council Directive 2003/109/EC to extend its scope to beneficiaries of international protection, O.J. L 132, 19.5.2011, p. 1

Regulation (EU) 492/2011 of the European Parliament and of the Council of 5 April 2011 on freedom of movement for workers within the Union, O.J. L 141, 27.5.2011, p. 1

Directive 2011/95/EU of the European Parliament and of the Council of 13 December 2011 on standards for the qualification of third-country nationals or stateless persons as beneficiaries of international protection, for a uniform status for refugees or for persons eligible for subsidiary protection, and for the content of the protection granted (recast), O.J. L 337, 20.12.2011, p. 9

Directive 2011/98/EU of the European Parliament and of the Council of 13 December 2011 on a single application procedure for a single permit for third-country nationals to reside and work in the territory of a Member State and on a common set of rights for third-country workers legally residing in a Member State, O.J. L 343, 23.12.2011, p. 1

Regulation (EU) 604/2013 of the European Parliament and of the Council of 26 June 2013 establishing the criteria and mechanisms for determining the Member State responsible for examining an application for international protection lodged in one of the Member States by a third-country national or a stateless person (recast), O.J. L 180, 29.6.2013, p. 31

Directive 2013/32/EU of the European Parliament and of the Council of 26 June 2013 on common procedures for granting and withdrawing international protection (recast), O.J. L 180, 29.6.2013, p. 60

Directive 2014/36/EU of the European Parliament and of the Council of 26 February 2014 on the conditions of entry and stay of third-country nationals for the purpose of employment as seasonal workers, O.J. L 94, 28.3.2014, p. 375

Directive 2014/54/EU of the European Parliament and of the Council of 16 April 2014 on measures facilitating the exercise of rights conferred on workers in the context of freedom of movement for workers, O.J. L 128, 30.4.2014, p. 8

Agreement between the European Union and the Republic of Turkey on the readmission of persons residing without authorisation, O.J. L 134, 7.5.2014, p. 3

Directive 2014/66/EU of the European Parliament and of the Council of 15 May 2014 on the conditions of entry and residence of third-country nationals in the framework of an intra-corporate transfer, O.J. L 157, 27.5.2014, p. 1

European Council, 'EU-Turkey statement', 18 March 2016

Regulation (EU) 2016/399 of the European Parliament and of the Council of 9 March 2016 on a Union Code on the rules governing the movement of persons across borders (Schengen Borders Code) (codification), O.J. L 77, 23.3.2016, p. 1

Directive (EU) 2016/801 of the European Parliament and of the Council of 11 May 2016 on the conditions of entry and residence of third-country nationals for the purposes of research, studies, training, voluntary service, pupil exchange schemes or educational projects and au pairing, O.J. L 132, 21.5.2016, p. 21

Regulation (EU) 2016/794 of the European Parliament and of the Council of 11 May 2016 on the European Union Agency for Law Enforcement Cooperation (Europol) and replacing and repealing Council Decisions 2009/371/JHA, 2009/934/JHA, 2009/935/JHA, 2009/936/JHA and 2009/968/JHA, O.J. L 135, 24.5.2016, p. 53

Regulation (EU) 2017/1954 of the European Parliament and of the Council of 25 October 2017 amending Council Regulation (EC) No. 1030/2002 laying down a uniform format for residence permits for third-country nationals, O.J. L 286, 1.11.2017, p. 9

Report from the Commission to the European Parliament, the European Council and the Council, Seventh Report on the Progress made in the implementation of the EU-Turkey Statement, COM(2017) 470, 6 September 2017

Regulation (EU) 2018/1806 of the European Parliament and of the Council of 14 November 2018 listing the third countries whose nationals must be in possession of visas when crossing the external borders and those whose nationals are exempt from that requirement O.J. L 303 28.11.2018, p. 39

Regulation (EU) 2018/1861 of the European Parliament and of the Council of 28 November 2018 on the establishment, operation and use of the Schengen Information System (SIS) in the field of border checks, and amending the Convention implementing the Schengen Agreement, and amending and repealing Regulation (EC) No. 1987/2006, O.J. L 312, 7.12.2018, p. 14

Regulation (EU) 2019/1149 of the European Parliament and of the Council of 20 June 2019 establishing a European Labour Authority, amending Regulations (EC) No. 883/2004, (EU) No. 492/2011, and (EU) 2016/589 and repealing Decision (EU) 2016/344, O.J. L 186, 11.7.2019, p. 21

Directive (EU) 2019/1158 of the European Parliament and of the Council of 20 June 2019 on work-life balance for parents and carers and repealing Council Directive 2010/18/EU, O.J. L 188, 12.7.2019, p. 79.

Recommendations to national courts and tribunals in relation to the initiation of preliminary ruling proceedings, O.J. C 380, 8.11.2019, p. 1

Regulation (EU) 2019/1896 of 13 November 2019 on the European Border and Coast Guard, O.J. L 295, 14.11.2019, p. 1

European Commission, Joint Communication to the European Council, State of Play of EU – Turkey political, economic and trade relations, JOIN (2021) 8 final/2, 22 March 2021

Regulation (EU) 2021/1152 of the European Parliament and of the Council of 7 July 2021 amending Regulations (EC) No. 767/2008, (EU) 2017/2226, (EU) 2018/

1240, (EU) 2018/1860, (EU) 2018/1861 and (EU) 2019/817 as regards the establishment of the conditions for accessing other EU information systems for the purposes of the European Travel Information and Authorisation System, O.J. L 249, 14.7.2021, p. 15

Directive (EU) 2021/1883 of the European Parliament and of the Council of 20 October 2021 on the conditions of entry and residence of third-country nationals for the purpose of highly qualified employment, and repealing Council Directive 2009/50/EC, O.J. L 382, 28.10.2021, p. 1

Regulation (EU) 2021/2303 of the European Parliament and of the Council of 15 December 2021 on the European Union Agency for Asylum and repealing Regulation (EU) No. 439/2010, O.J. L 468, 30.12.2021, p. 1

Council Decision (EU) 2022/333 of 25 February 2022 on the partial suspension of the application of the Agreement between the European Community and the Russian Federation on the facilitation of the issuance of visas to the citizens of the European Union and the Russian Federation, O.J. L 54, 25.2.2022, p. 1

Council Decision (EU) 2022/1500 of 9 September 2022 on the suspension in whole of the application of the Agreement between the European Community and the Russian Federation on the facilitation of the issuance of visas to the citizens of the European Union and the Russian Federation, O.J. L 234I, 9.9.2022, p. 1

Commission Implementing Decision (EU) 2022/1945 of 21 February 2020 on documents to be issued by Member States pursuant to Article 18(1) and (4) and Article 26 of the Agreement on the withdrawal of the United Kingdom of Great Britain and Northern Ireland from the European Union and the European Atomic Energy Community (notified under document C(2020) 1114), C/2020/1114, O.J. L 268, 14.10.2022, p. 26

Council Directive (EU) 2022/2523 of 14 December 2022 on ensuring a global minimum level of taxation for multinational enterprise groups and large-scale domestic groups in the Union, O.J. L 328, 22.12.2022, p. 1

Regulation (EU) 2023/850 of the European Parliament and of the Council of 19 April 2023 amending Regulation (EU) 2018/1806 listing the third countries whose nationals must be in possession of visas when crossing the external borders and those whose nationals are exempt from that requirement (Kosovo (This designation is without prejudice to positions on status, and is in line with UNSCR 1244/1999 and the ICJ Opinion on the Kosovo declaration of independence.)), O.J. L 110, 25.4.2023, p. 1

Memorandum of Understanding on a strategic and global partnership between the European Union and Tunisia (16 July 2023)

European Commission, Commission Notice – Guidance on the right of free movement of EU citizens and their families, C/2023/8500, 22 December 2023

Directive 2024/505 of the European Parliament and of the Council of 7 February 2024 amending Directive 2005/36/EC as regards the recognition of professional qualifications of nurses responsible for general care trained in Romania, O.J. L, 2024/505, 12.2.2024

Regulation (EU) 2024/1717 of the European Parliament and of the Council of 13 June 2024 amending Regulation (EU) 2016/399 on a Union Code on the rules governing the movement of persons across borders, O.J. L, 2024/1717, 20.6.2024

European Parliament, Resolution of 7 February 2024 on the rule of law and media freedom in Greece

European Commission, Communication from the Commission to the European Parliament, the European Council and the Council, *Striking a balance on migration: an approach that is both fair and firm*, Brussels, 12 March 2024, COM(2024) 126 final

Joint Declaration on the Strategic and Comprehensive Partnership between the Arab Republic of Egypt and the European Union (17 March 2024)

**3. Bilateral agreements, multilateral treaties and other international documents (in alphabetical order) [where applicable, the Greek ratification instruments appear in brackets]**

Agreement between the European Community and its Member States, of the one part, and the Swiss Confederation, of the other, on the free movement of persons (1999)

Agreement between the Government of the Hellenic Republic and the Government of the Arab Republic of Egypt on the Employment of Seasonal workers in the Agricultural Sector (2022) [Law 5009/2023, FEK 2023 Issue A' No. 7]

Agreement between the Government of the Hellenic Republic and the Council of Ministers of Albania for the protection and assistance of children victims of trafficking (2006) [Law 3692/2008, FEK 2008 Issue A' No. 173]

Agreement between the Governments of the States of the Benelux Economic Union, the Federal Republic of Germany and the French Republic on the gradual abolition of checks at their common borders (1985) [Law 2514/1997 FEK 1997 Issue A' No. 140]

Convention Implementing the Schengen Agreement (1990) [Law 2514/1997 FEK 1997 Issue A' No. 140]

Agreement between the Hellenic Republic and the Arab Republic of Egypt for the promotion of bilateral cooperation concerning labour matters (1981) [Law 1453/1984 of 14 June 1984, FEK 1984 Issue A' No. 88]

Agreement of 23 April 1948 between the Hellenic Government and the Government of the United States of America [Law 3152/1955, FEK 1955 Issue A' No. 64]

Agreement of Seasonal Employment of Labour Force between the Government of the Hellenic Republic and the Government of the Republic of Bulgaria (1995) [Law 2407/1996, FEK 1996 Issue A' No. 103]

Agreement of Seasonal Employment of Labour Force between the Government of the Hellenic Republic and the Government of the Republic of Albania (1996) [Law 2482/1997, FEK 1997 Issue A' No. 73]

Convention against Torture and Other Cruel, Inhuman or Degrading Treatment or Punishment, (1984) [Law 1782/1988, FEK 1988 Issue A' No. 116]

Convention concerning Discrimination in Respect of Employment and Occupation (1958, ILO Convention No. 111) [Law 1424/1984, FEK 1984 Issue A' No. 29]

Convention concerning Freedom of Association and Protection of the Right to Organise (1950, ILO Convention No. 87) [Legislative Decree 4204/1961, FEK 1961 Issue A' No. 174]

## Table of Legislation

Convention concerning the Application of the Principles of the Right to Organise and to Bargain Collectively (1949, ILO Convention No. 98) [Legislative Decree 4205/1961, FEK 1961 Issue A' No. 174]

Convention for the Protection of Human Rights and Fundamental Freedoms ((ETS No. 005, 1950) [Legislative Decree 53/1974, FEK 1974 Issue A' 256]

Protocol No. 4 to the Convention for the Protection of Human Rights and Fundamental Freedoms securing certain rights and freedoms other than those already included in the Convention and in the first Protocol thereto (ETS No. 046, 1963)

Protocol No. 7 to the Convention for the Protection of Human Rights and Fundamental Freedoms ((ETS No. 117, 1984) [Law 1705/1987, FEK 1987 Issue A' No. 89]

Protocol No. 12 to the Convention for the Protection of Human Rights and Fundamental Freedoms (ETS No. 177, 2000)

Convention of 22 April 1980 between the Hellenic Republic and the United States of America [Law 1982/1991, FEK 1991 Issue A' No. 188]

Convention on the Participation of Foreigners in Public Life at Local Level (ETS No. 144, 1992)

Convention on the Reduction of Statelessness (1961)

Convention relating to the Status of Refugees (1951) [Legislative Decree 3989/1959, FEK 1959 Issue A' No. 201]

Protocol relating to the Status of Refugees (1967) [Compulsory Law 389/1968, FEK 1968 Issue A' No. 125]

Convention relating to the Status of Stateless Persons (1954) [Law 139/1975, FEK 1975 Issue A' No. 176]

Council of Europe Convention on Action against Trafficking in Human Beings (CETS No. 197, 2005) [Law 4216/2013, FEK 2013 Issue A' No. 266]

Council of European Convention against Trafficking in Human Organs (CETS No. 216, 2015)

Equal Remuneration Convention (1951, ILO Convention No. 100) [Law 46/1975, FEK 1975 Issue A' No. 105]

European Agreement on Regulations governing the Movement of Persons between Member States of the Council of Europe (ETS No. 25, 1957) [Law 4077/1960, FEK 1960 Issue A' No. 106]

European Agreement on the Abolition of Visas for Refugees (ETS No. 31, 1959)

European Agreement on Transfer of Responsibility for Refugees (ETS No. 107, 1980)

European Convention on Establishment (ETS No. 019, 1955) [ratified in 1965]

European Convention on the Legal Status of Migrant Workers (ETS No. 93, 1977)

European Social Charter ((ETS No. 035, 1961) [Law 1426/1984, FEK 1984 Issue A' No. 32]

Additional Protocol to the European Social Charter (ETS No. 128) 1988 [Law 2595/1998, FEK 1998 Issue A' No. 63]

Additional Protocol to the European Social Charter Providing for a System of Collective Complaints (ETS No. 158) 1995 [Law 2595/1998, FEK 1998 Issue A' No. 63]

International Covenant on Civil and Political Rights (1966) [Law 2462/1997, FEK 1997 Issue A' No. 25]

International Labour Organization, International Standard Classification of Occupations, ISCO-08. Structure, Group Definitions and Correspondence Tables (2012)
Memorandum of Understanding between Greece and Australia (Work and Holiday Visa) [Law 4353/2015, FEK 2015 Issue A' No. 173]
Memorandum of Understanding between the Government of the Hellenic Republic and the Government of the People's Republic of Bangladesh on Migration and Mobility (2022) [Law 4959/2022, FEK 2022 Issue A' No. 144]
Agreement between the Government of the Hellenic Republic and the Government of the Arab Republic of Egypt on the Employment of Seasonal workers in the Agricultural Sector (2022) [Law 5009/2023, FEK 2023 Issue A' No. 7]
New York Convention on the Status of Stateless Persons (1954) [Law 139/1975, FEK 1975, Issue A', No. 176]
Protocol to United Nations Convention against Transnational Organized Crime to Prevent, Suppress and Punish Trafficking in Persons, especially Women and Children (2000) [Law 3875/2010, FEK 2010 A' No. 158]
Statute of the International Criminal Court (1998) [Law 3003/2002 FEK 2002 Issue A' No. 75]
Trade and Cooperation Agreement between the European Union and the European Atomic Energy Community, of the one part, and the United Kingdom of Great Britain and Northern Ireland, of the other part (2020)
Treaty on European Union (Treaty of Lisbon) (2007) [Law 3671/2008, FEK 2008 Issue A' No. 129]
Treaty on the Functioning of the European Union (Treaty of Lisbon) (2007) [Law 3671/2008, FEK 2008 Issue A' No. 129]
UN Human Rights Council, Report of the Independent Expert on the effects of foreign debt and other related international financial obligations of States on the full enjoyment of all human rights, particularly economic, social and cultural rights, Cephas Lumina, Mission to Greece (22–27 April 2013), UN Doc. A/HRC/25/50/Add.1, 7 March 2014
United Nations International Convention on the Protection of the Rights of All Migrant Workers and Members of their Families (1990)
Universal Declaration of Human Rights (UN General Assembly Resolution 217 A (III), 1948)
Vienna Convention on Consular Relations (1963) [Law 90/1975, FEK 1975 Issue A' No. 150]
Vienna Convention on Diplomatic Relations (1961) [Legislative Decree 503/1970, FEK 1970 Issue A' No. 108]

# Table of International Case Law (in Alphabetical Order)

*A.D. v. Greece*, ECtHR, Application No. 55363/19, Judgment of 4 April 2023

*Alkhatib et autres c. Grèce*, ECtHR, Application No. 3566/16Judgment, 16 January 2024

*Elliniko Symvoulio gia tous Prosfyges and Ypostirixi Prosfygon sto Aigaio*, CJEU, Case C-134/23, Judgment, 4 October 2024, ECLI:EU:C:2024:838

*Ermira Bajratari v. Secretary of State for the Home Department*, CJEU, Case C-93/18, Judgment, 2 October 2019, ECLI:EU:C:2019:809

*GV v. Chief Appeals Officer and Others*, CJEU, Case C-488/21, Judgment, 21 December 2023, ECLI:EU:C:2023:1013

*M.B. v. Greece*, ECtHR, Application No. 8389/20, Judgment, 23 November 2023

*M.L. v. Greece*, ECtHR, Application No. 8386/20, Judgment, 23 November 2023

*NF and Others v. European Council,* CJEU, Joined Cases C-208/17 P to C-210/17 P, Order, 12 September 2018, ECLI:EU:C:2018:705

*NF v. European Council*, CJEU, Case T-192/16, Order, 28 February 2017, EU:T:2017:128

*NG v. European Council*, CJEU, Case T-193/16, Order, 28 February 2017, EU:T:2017:129

*NM v. European Council*, CJEU, Case T-257/16, Order, 28 February 2017, EU:T:2017:130

*Safi and Others v. Greece*, ECtHR, Application No. 5418/15, Judgment, 7 July 2022

# Index

*The numbers here refer to paragraph numbers.*

## Index

www.ingramcontent.com/pod-product-compliance
Lightning Source LLC
Chambersburg PA
CBHW071347230926
51846CB00002B/470
* 9 7 8 9 4 0 3 5 4 4 3 9 7 *